D1218117

1968
Magnum
throughout
the world

MAGNUM
PHOTOS

1968 Magnum throughout the world

texts by Eric Hobsbawm
and Marc Weitzmann

HAZAN

Art editor :
Agnès Sire
with Delphine Desveaux
for the picture research
Design and production :
Atalante/Paris
Editor :
Stéphanie Grégoire
Translation :
Dominique Lablanche and Antoine Hazan
Chronology :
Aurélien Moline
Correction :
Christine Monnet
Project management :
François Hébel

Litho origination :
Prodima, Bilbao
Printing :
Castuera, Pampelune

The publication of this book will be
accompanied by an exhibition at the
Sorbonne in Paris, which will then be
presented elsewhere in France and overseas.
This exhibition is sponsored by :
**RFI Radio France Internationale,
Canon Photo,
Kodak Professionnel,
Pictorial Service,
INA Institut national de l'audiovisuel,
Mission pour la photographie
du ministère de la Culture
et de la Communication,
Scam.**

Exhibition tour management :
Diane Auberger with Mika Sato.

**Magnum would like to thank
the following for their contribution :**
Mesdames Michèle Gendreau-Massaloux,
Marie-Charlotte Bolot, Christine Berbudeau,
Agnès de Gouvion-Saint-Cyr, Marylin Passini,
Natasha Dzikowski, Pascale Froment,
Junko Ogawa, Liz Grogan.
Messieurs Pascal Briard, Edy Gassman,
François Eschapasse, Guy Bourreau,
Nicolas Sire, Henry Chapier,
Jean-Luc Monterosso, René Backmann,
Pierre Guillemin, Georges Vercheval,
Josef Koudelka, René Burri, Chris Boot,
Peter Spier, and l'atelier Circad.

TABLE OF CONTENTS

THE YEAR THE PROPHETS FAILED

Eric Hobsbawm

The last thing that their politicians, or even their established intellectuals, envisaged, were riots in cities like Paris and the apparently sudden conversion of a mass of young middle class men and women to the revolutionary cause.

History does not usually suit the convenience of people who like to separate it into neat periods, but there are times when it seems to have pity on them. 1968 is an important date in the history of all the three worlds into which observers liked to divide the globe in the era of the Cold War: the "first world" of western capitalism, the "second world" of the communist states and the "third world" of Asia, Africa and Latin America. It might almost have been designed to serve as some sort of historical landmark.

None of those of us who lived through the year 1968 will ever forget it. For all of us it contains public events which moved us in the way in which Americans — but not only they — remember being moved by the assassination of President Kennedy. We remember them, not simply as a newspaper headline or TV images, but as part of the fabric of our personal lives. As I write, I can see the great, street-filling torrent of the Paris student demonstrations in early May, carrying with it somehow, in formal suit and tie, the respectable historian of the French Revolution, my friend Albert Soboul, deeply disapproving of counterculture and the heterodox left, but morally compelled to march "quand le peuple descend dans la rue." I see myself, walking up a bare Welsh valley on an August morning, desperate and incredulous after the radio news of the Soviet invasion of Czechoslovakia. Say "1968" and we who were of age at that time are plunged back into that extraordinary year.

On the other hand those for whom 1968 is a living memory are today middle-aged or old. To have been alive at all in 1968 a person has to be thirty years old today. Hardly anyone below the age of forty-five can genuinely regard the great year as part of their conscious lives. So, for the benefit of the post-1968 generations, it may be useful to begin by reminding ourselves what actually happened during those remarkable twelve months.

Almost all of it was unexpected. The economies of the Western countries were at the peak of what French observers were to call "les trente glorieuses," the greatest era of prosperity and growth in the history of the industrialized world. The last thing that their politicians, or even their established intellectuals, envisaged, were riots in cities like Paris and the apparently sudden conversion of a mass of young middle class men and women to the revolutionary cause. The last thing anyone expected then, inside or outside the communist world, was what happened in Czechoslovakia: a Communist Party in government officially converting to a tolerant pluralism. It was already possible to predict that the USA, with all its global power, would not be able to maintain itself permanently in Vietnam, but who even at Christmas 1967, predicted the Tet offensive and its almost instantaneous impact on the domestic politics of the United States?

This apparent suddenness and unexpectedness made the events of 1968 so startling and dramatic. There were plenty of such events... The year began with the North Vietnamese Tet offensive which, as we now know, broke the determination of the USA, and made its defeat in Vietnam certain. It led almost immediately to President Lindon. Johnson's decision not to stand for re-election, largely under the pressure of student anti-war demonstrations. This, in consequence, led to the election of Richard Nixon as president of the United States that same year. At about the same time Alexander Dubcek took over the leadership of the Czechoslovak Communist Party. The resignation of President Novotny was followed by the reforms of the "Prague Spring" which attempted to establish "communism with a human face." On August 20-21 the Dubcek regime was overpowered by the Soviet invasion of the Czechoslovak Republic. The triumph of the reformers in Prague produced student demonstrations in Poland, which were severely repressed. The dominant, ultra-nationalist group in the Polish government blamed the demonstrations on the Jews. Most of the few thousand Jews still remaining in the country were driven out.

Spring was also the season of crisis in France. The so called "events of May" were not only the largest student mobilisation in French history, but they also broadened into what was possibly its largest general strike... Whether or not this extraordinary upheaval could have turned into the first peace-time revolution in Western Europe since Spain in 1936 was much debated at the time. Probably not. However, though General de Gaulle survived the crisis, his retirement a year later was certainly the direct, if delayed, consequence of May 1968, and so, probably, was the restoration of the Union of the Left under a common program in the early 1970s. The French "events of May" were almost immediately followed in Yugoslavia by massive student demonstrations in favor of reform. President Tito was, however, wise enough to appease the students on June 9. The fact that the student movement occurred almost simultaneously east and west of what was called "the iron curtain" is one of the most significant and unexpected aspects of 1968.

The student movement was not confined to the West. In the autumn when the drama shifted back across the Atlantic, this time to Mexico, its most spectacular episode was the massacre of students and others at a great public meeting in Mexico City shortly before the opening of the Olympic Games. the meeting was the culmination of a majo

Historians who lived through 1968 were inevitably reminded of another year described in terms of seasonal poetry as "the springtime of people," 1848, the year of European revolution. Like 1848, 1968 raised enormous, often romantic hopes. Like 1848, it also ended in disappointment.

student and popular agitation in that country. Though it was immediately met by ruthless repression, it is significant that Mexican government policy moved to the left under the next president, Luis Echeverria Alvarez (who, as Minister of the Interior, had been responsible for the repression).

Another unexpected development occurred in Latin America. The death of Che Guevara in 1967 had marked the end of the illjudged Cuban attempt to spread Fidel Castro's revolution by exporting guerrilla war to the continent, and, incidentally, turned the image of Che into a universal political icon. However, the place of guerrillas now seemed to be taken by progressive, anti-imperialist military coups. (Conservative coups were familiar enough, in and out of Latin America: i.e., in Brazil and in Greece.) The one in Panama by General Omar Torrijos was to lead to a sharp and longlasting confrontation with the USA. The more important one in Peru by a junta under General Velasco was to lead to the most far-reaching agrarian reform ever undertaken by a non-revolutionary regime in the western hemisphere.

Finally, returning to Europe we see the start of the "Troubles" in Northern Ireland with the clash between police and civil rights demonstrators in Londonderry. In Western Germany the attempted assassination of the student leader Rudi Dutschke initiated the phase of massive student agitation in that country, while in Italy the combination of student demonstrations and riots with a 24-hour general strike already announced the great termoil which was to reach its peak in the so called "hot autumn" of 1969.

These events were dramatic enough, even if we do not include those which made the headlines but probably had less far-reaching consequences, such as the assassinations of Martin Luther King and Senator Robert Kennedy the – as usual unexpected – uprising in Watts the "Negro" quarter of prosperous Los Angeles, or those symbolic acts of African-American radicalization, the clenched-fist salutes of black athletes at the Olympic Games. However, it is important to bear in mind at least four developments, which cannot be identified with any particular date in 1968, but which continued through-out the year and left their mark on it.

The first of these was Mao's Great Cultural Revolution in China, which was reaching its peak. It is an episode which the Chinese people would prefer to forget, but in the West, where little was known about China, it inspired a short-lived fashion for "Maoism," mainly among youthful intellectuals attracted by the Great Helmsman's calls for continuous revolution.

The second was the continued conflict in the Middle East. After the Israeli victory in the Six Day War of 1967, armed action by Palestinian commandoes was increasingly visible, as was counter-terrorism by the Israelis.

The third was the tragic civil war in Nigeria, arising out of the attempted secession of one of its regions in 1967. It dragged on throughout 1968 until the inevitable defeat of the diplomatically isolated secessionist Biafra.

Finally, and both visible and audible, there was the counter-cultural upheaval which was the great cultural revolution of the western world. 1967-69 were the years of the major rock festivals –from Monterey to Woodstock and Altamont – and 1968 was its epicentre.

Historians who lived through 1968 were inevitably reminded of another year described in terms of seasonal poetry as "the springtime of people," 1848, the year of European revolution. Like 1848, 1968 raised enormous, often romantic hopes. Like 1848, it also ended in disappointment; the dramatic events on the public scene appeared to achieve very little. Perhaps that is one reason why 1968 lent itself so well to photographic reporting.

Photography catches the living moment, which is how people experience history, but not historical consequences; although Magnum has been better than any other group of photographers at catching the historic tone and the contemporary mood of the occasion. At its best, perhaps even more brilliantly, these pictures concentrate into a single image the contradictions and complexities of situations, as in Don McCullin's Biafran carrying a load of artillery shells on her head like a bunch of bananas. Or in Henri Cartier-Bresson's *petit bourgeois* contemplating the posters and graffiti of the Parisian walls of May. Still, inevitably these are images which can only hint at context and ignore consequence. Had photography been invented in time for the Napoleonic Wars, the Magnum photographer would have seen the battle of Waterloo, had he or she been present, as Stendhal's Fabrice saw it in *La Chartreuse de Parme* rather than like Napoleon, or Wellington, or Talleyrand… In any case Magnum's hypothetical ancestor would almost certainly have found the decision-makers at the top visually less interesting, except as equestrian portraits, than action on the ground. But who, in 1968, made the big decisions? The most characteristic movements of 1968 idealised spontaneity and were opposed to leadership, structure and strategy. Their natural ideology should have been anarchism, rather than the images of Marx, Lenin, Mao and Che which the politically conscious among them preferred. The natural weapon of rebellion in 1968 was neither the gun nor the political resolution but the graffitti-filled wall, the improvised poster and the microphone.

Yet it is a mistake to treat 1968 as though it had been a year of failed revolution, or, in the words of the historian's bon-mot about 1848 "a turning-point when Europe failed to turn." At best it was a reminder that the foundations of the economic golden age in the West were subsiding; as were those of the centrally planned economies of the Soviet type, whose deficiencies were increasingly evident. Still, in the East, as the defeat of the Prague Spring by the tanks of the USSR showed, the time for the disintegration of the Soviet empire had not yet come, although after August 1968 it was evident that only the readiness of Moscow to intervene, kept it stable.

In the developed countries of the West the golden age of economic growth and Keynesian welfare politics ended sooner — 1973 marks the major turning-point — but nobody as yet expected it to end. None of the major political movements, and certainly not the European socialist parties, seriously counted on a change of economic regime, and most did not even envisage it. In the West the student rebellion, though it appeared to talk the language of politics, was a phenomenon outside economics and politics. Apart from its contribution to the fight against the Vietnam war, its impact on politics and industrial unrest was unintended. Its cultural significance in the developed capitalist countries was far greater than its political significance, unlike analogous movements in the communist countries and other dictatorships…

In fact, it is the eruption of cultural change after two decades of unprecedented economic and social transformation that makes 1968 a significant date in the history of the 20th century. It dramatized the educational revolution which, in all three worlds, was turning university students from small middle-class elites into vast armies. In France their numbers more than tripled to 650,000 in the 1960s. It dramatized the globalization of communications, which spread the same icons, the same banners, from campus to campus across continents and oceans within weeks. It dramatized the unprecedented prosperity, translated into the purchasing-power of an emerging social stratum of "youth," who were culturally and economically autonomous. The record industry could now rely for 75 % of its income on rock-music which appealed overwhelmingly to the age groups from 14 to 24. It dramatized the widening gap between the traditions and modes of behavior, the hopes, fears and expectations, of the pre-1950 and the post-1950 generations. Above all, perhaps, it dramatized the sheer *extent* of the change in public and private social behavior, as in the relation between generations and sexes, which was taking place in the 1960s. This, after all, was the decade when: the French women's clothing industry, for the first time, produced more trousers than skirts; of the rapid fall in the choice of the Catholic priesthood as a vocation; of a militantly dissident counter-culture.

These were not political phenomena in the traditional sense, though, like all major socio-economic and cultural changes, they engendered a political fall-out and were expressed, among other idioms, in the established language of politics, as they still are. Yet, though the rhetoric of 1968 did not clearly distinguish between making love, dropping acid and making revolution, the conversion of John Lennon after 1968 to a sort of political radicalism, which led the FBI to accumulate a large file about him, is one of the less significant aspects of the phonomenon of rock music in general and The Beatles in particular. What 1968 made visible (spectacularly so in the West, less dramatically in the world of communist Europe, less still in the Third World), was the extraordinary acceleration of social transformation in the post-1945 decades which historians will recognize as the most revolutionary in world history.

This, after all, was the decade: when the French women's clothing industry, for the first time, produced more trousers than skirts; of the rapid fall in the choice of the Catholic priesthood; of a militantly dissident counter-culture.

THE YEAR COCA-COLA WON THE COLD WAR

Marc Weitzmann

This was a mass-produced celebration of banality as the embodiment of modern identity. It was the quest for lyricism in the most banal and the most trivial of everyday events.

When Spike Lee's movie *Do the Right Thing* was released, the lead actress, Rosie Perez, told an interviewer that her director had led her to discover — along with other features of contemporary culture — the old records of "that little guy who sings like a duck, what's he called?" That was in 1991. Before meeting Lee, Perez had never heard the voice, or even the name, of Bob Dylan (for it was he, of course). Oh yeah, yeah, that's it, Bob Whosit.

Twenty-three years earlier, Dylan's songs were on everyone's lips — so much so that in the course of 1968 one of them gave its name to the very first urban guerrilla movement, the Weathermen ("You don't need a weatherman to know which way the wind blows," *Subterranean Homesick Blues*). Looking at those photographs now, it is hard not to find the tunes running in your head. With their savage, black irony, unthinkable now; with their ambiguous Messianic message and their strong hint of despair; with the faint whiff of drugs that clouded the singer's voice (liberation or suicide?); with their 1950s-style drumming, their journeyman guitar-picking, and, above all, perhaps, the strictly who-gives-a-damn atmosphere of the whole thing — who nowadays would dare to punctuate a number with a burst of laughter or a coughing fit? These songs are the best reflection of a distant age when anything seemed possible, and when what you hoped for never happened.

More years now separate us from 1968 than separated 1968 from the end of World War II. Then, we were still in a postwar phase; indeed, maybe that was when the postwar phase ended. It was the first year of an era which, for better or worse, is with us still. It marked a threshold, and that explains its fascination. It is us, and yet it is not. It was the time of the first, giant stadium gigs. On records, the first tracks longer than the regulation three minutes had come out earlier in the decade; that was Dylan's influence, again. Youth was virgin territory, discovering itself. There was no rock marketing, no Levi's ad campaigns, no merchandising; the entertainment industry had yet to institutionalize rule-breaking, musical or other. It all seemed very new, and — very unlike the present day — a lot of things really were new. One day a census of the objects that first appeared between 1968 and the end of the century will have to be taken. In 1968 color TV barely existed; supermarkets were still rare, in Europe at all events, and they still carried an aura of novelty and rich profusion. Most of the disposable objects that are all around us now — from plastic bottles to sneakers, from badges to backpacks, from tee-shirts to throwaway ballpoints (forbidden for school use in France): it was all still new.

Leonard Cohen, Allen Ginsberg, and above all Andy Warhol, who were among the best interpreters of what was happening then, were finding poetic uses for all of this supposedly vulgar, trashy material. Warhol's celebrated phrase, "In the future everyone will be famous for fifteen minutes," had its origin in the vast 1960s influx of new, inanimate objects. The Warhol exhibition at the Rowan Gallery, London, in March 1968, was a celebration of Campbell's soup cans, Brillo boxes, and helium-filled cushions; and his films, screened in the same year, were nonstop, unedited images of things like a man sleeping, or the Empire State Building. This was a mass-produced celebration of banality as the embodiment of modern identity. It was the quest for lyricism in the most banal and the most trivial of everyday events. While this wholesale invasion of our personal space was in progress, the most distant parts of the globe were coming within our reach. This was the time when airplane tickets reached the mass market. The development of charter flights, as well as that of the communications media, launched the process of cultural hybridization in which we are now more deeply immersed than ever. Cuba, India, China — destinations unthinkable for most would-be travelers, even ten years earlier — became accessible to almost anyone who could summon up the courage.

The Third World had its awakening at the turn of the 1960s, and it still held the promise of possible alternative lifestyles. In a sense, Frantz Fanon's analysis of the processes of assimilation, freedom-fighting and de-colonization served as a metaphor for all of those in the industrialized countries who were now trying to "liberate" themselves. Now, when people traveled, it was not so much to export their own humanitarian values to barbaric countries as to discover other types of consciousness. As seen from the vantage point of a Western culture that was caught up in a process of constant expansion, the world seemed both far more unified and far more diverse than it does now. It was rich, it was vast, and for the time being — despite the best efforts of the major oil and fruit corporations and of the cultural industries — there was none of the cultural and political uniformity that those bodies (and the Web) are imposing now. Most of the coups d'état intended to remedy this situation did not take place until the 1970s. It really was another world, back in 1968.

Civilizations remote from the West were perceived both as revolutionary and as ancestral: it was possible, without apparent contradiction, to sing the praises both of Communist China and of the classics of Chinese literature that the regime was censoring. And so, in February 1968, while the Tet offensive was raging in Vietnam, the Beatles — surely the symbolic representatives of all those young people who were demonstrating against the war – had no compunction in flying off to the Himalayas to absorb the teachings of Love dispensed by Maharishi Mahesh Yogi, President of the Academy of Transcendental Meditation. "I don't care about the political situation," said John Lennon on his return. "I don't give a toss whether the Greek government [then recently taken over by the Colonels] is totally Fascist or totally Communist." Ringo Starr went one step farther, with a declaration that would not have been disowned by the devotees of the New Right thirty years later: "The government turns everything it touches to shit. The railways made money when they were private, didn't they?"

It was an age of flamboyant contradictions, of mindless hedonism and ideological revolt, of resolute optimism and of trips to hell (whether hell went by the name of Saigon, Prague or LSD). Let the bombs fall, urged Jeff Nuttall in an apologia for drugs (*Bomb Culture*, 1968), evoking the image of a giant mandala that unfolds in the infinitesimal moment when everything that can be will be. Why bother, he mused, with the world and the human race? They were not real, in any case.

It was an age of flamboyant contradictions, of mindless hedonism and ideological revolt, of resolute optimism and of trips to hell (whether hell went by the name of Saigon, Prague or LSD).

What was going on?

In Italy, on March 1, clashes between police and students paralyzed the city of Rome and left 200 injured, of whom 147 were policemen. In the following months, the revolt spread to Pisa, Milan, Florence, Naples, Venice, Trento, and Palermo. The country's overcrowded universities suffered $100 million worth of damage.

In Spain, at the end of that same month, the student movement, allied to Communist, Socialist and Anarchist labor organizations, organized massive demonstrations to protest both the Vietnam War and the Franco regime that had ruled Spain for nearly thirty years. Almost 175,000 striking students confronted the Guardia Civil all through the spring of the year.

In West Germany, the mass anti-Vietnam War protests organized by the students of the German League of Socialist Students (SDS) met with great hostility from the population at large. In Berlin in February, crowds turned on the students and pursued them with cries of "Give them a haircut! Lynch them! String them up!" Two months later, on April 11 (just six days after the assassination of Martin Luther King in Memphis, Tennessee), one Joseph Bachmann fired two bullets into the head of the German student leader, Rudi Dutschke. Fierce rioting broke out in all the main West German cities. In May, to tame the rioters, the Bundestag voted emergency laws that evoked some sinister memories. They did not work.

In France François Missoffe, the Minister for Youth and Sport, who had written a voluminous report on young people, was publicly criticized by a student, Daniel Cohn-Bendit, for leaving sexual issues out of his report. Missoffe advised a cold dip as the best remedy; Cohn-Bendit retorted that this was the answer he would have expected from a spokesman for the Hitler Youth. Expulsion proceedings against Cohn-Bendit were started. In reply, a thousand students sat in at Nanterre University and defied the police, chanting: "Professors, you're old, and so is your culture." That was the birth of the March 22 Movement.

In London, the Grosvenor Square demonstration, in which nearly 25,000 people took part, got out of hand. Those injured included 117 policemen and 45 demonstrators, there were 246 arrests. In April, a British Conservative politician, Enoch Powell, fanned the flames with a racist speech, denouncing the folly of admitting "50,000 immigrants" every year to swell the numbers of ethnic minorities. Two months earlier, the Labor government, yielding to pressure, had introduced annual immigration quotas and had limited the right of entry enjoyed by the bearers of certain categories of British passport. This openly racist law had unleashed a bitter public debate, and Powell's speech made things worse. Riots broke out. On and off, all through the spring, students led by Tariq Ali clashed on the streets of London with the proletarians of the Smithfield and Billingsgate provision markets, who supported the government's racist policy.

In the United States, there was a heady mixture of anti-Vietnam War sentiment, race war and social conflict. An official survey revealed that, of the 234 sons of Senators and Representatives who were of military age, only twenty-eight had actually entered the armed forces since the beginning of the war, and only one had been wounded. Most GIs were from the ghettos, or else from the blue-collar white families of the Midwest and of cities like Baltimore.

In 1968, cracks appeared along all of these fault lines at once. In Vietnam, the Tet offensive in February and the My Lai massacre in March carried the war into a new and more savage phase. In the U.S., on the race front, the murder of Martin Luther King on April 5 and, on the very next day, the violent arrest of a leading Black Panther figure, the writer Eldridge Cleaver, turned the emphasis from civil rights to something approaching civil war. During the arrest, one of Cleaver's friends was killed by police. Riots broke out in over a hundred cities, leaving 309 dead and more than 2,500 injured. Twenty days later, students sat in at Columbia University, New York, amid cries of "Make One, Two, Three Columbias" – an adaptation of one of the Che Guevara's slogans. Clashes with police left 68 people injured, and nearly 800 under arrest. In June, Robert Kennedy, who was seeking

Presidential nomination as the last champion of the liberal left against Nixon, was himself assassinated.

All over the world – in Japan, Mexico and elsewhere – there were student demonstrations accompanied by extremes of violence. The list could go on indefinitely.

What was going on? Where did all this rebellious energy, evident all over the planet, come from? When we look beyond the slogans and the events themselves, what strikes us now in the photographs of those protests is the activity, the physical energy of those concerned. They have an almost filmic mobility, and this is not merely an impression created by skillful photography. Just make the comparison with some more recent photographs, such as those of current demonstrations against the extreme right in France. Nowadays, most of the demonstrators keep in line, with their bodies concealed behind their banners; or else they troop along in more or less densely compacted masses, conducting a procession from A to B and reciting their slogans. In 1968, on the other hand, the bodies speak for themselves; they speak just as clearly as the banners, if not more so. Every individual body is on the move and seems to say what the people of Prague said to the Russian soldiers who invaded the city in August 1968: "Look me in the eye!"

Whether at a street protest for sexual equality in New York, or in the Sorbonne sit-in, or even on a Gaullist march, everyone present invests the picture with a powerful, speaking, physical presence. You can often tell from the way they talk to each other that they disagree, but that is beside the point: they are part of a movement full of contradictions, in which nothing is yet set in stone.

And in 1968 that movement was everywhere. In the theater, people were starting to regard the author's written text as an abuse of authority. To hell with Chekhov, to hell with Shakespeare, as one actor put it. Under the influence of the Living Theater, led by Julian Beck and Judith Malina, the stage had turned into "guerrilla theater," or "gestural theater," in which performers would, for instance, come along and die on top of members of the audience, or insult them, or threaten them, or even undress them, with cries of "What are you doing for Vietnam? What are you doing for Black people?" Other options were to examine their mouths, or to paint them. Bodies were what counted. The stage had given way to vast Happenings, which shaded off into street protests. Anything could happen.

Though the results were theatrically disastrous in most cases – at least according to conventional artistic criteria – stage plays had ceased to be shows and had turned into ways of taking action. "Of late," wrote a contemporary critic, "audience participation has grown to a point where one fully expects to go to the theater one evening and get laid right there."

Sexual liberation, artistic liberation, political liberation, racial liberation: in all of these, the individual body was at the fore. Not without a great deal of rampant machismo, it must be added. This was the year that saw the appearance of underground hardcore magazines such as Konkret in Germany and Screw in the United States. And the Black Panthers (though sticklers for propriety in their own family lives) famously decreed that the appropriate position for women in the revolutionary movement was "prone." The feminists were not to be outdone. In an event that came somewhere between a theatrical happening and a political protest, one movement, WITCH (Women's Inter-national Terrorist Con-

spiracy), intoned their ancestral maledictions from the floor of the New York Stock Exchange.

What was going on? Contrary to general belief, all this rebellious energy cannot – or cannot exclusively – be explained by the youth of those involved. It derived, rather, from the encounter between all those young people and the spectacular moral support they received from the great intellectuals of the day. It is likely that a considerable part of the rebels' sheer audacity, and their radicalism, sprang from the forthright encouragement provided by Jean-Paul Sartre, Jean Genet, Herbert Marcuse, Noam Chomsky and the rest. Bertrand Russell, a winner of the Nobel Prize for literature, publicly ripped up his British Labor Party membership card and condemned, on air, the "disgusting opportunism" of the Party's leaders. Can any equivalent be imagined today? And where is the intellectual with sufficient symbolic prestige to do it?

This is what we see in the photographs: the absence of fear and guilt, and the determination to act. Intellectuals had no fear of breaking decisively with what are now called the "parties in power" – the phrase people use today to designate the impotence of those in office. In the United States, Dr. Benjamin Spock, pediatrician and author of one of the most phenomenal best-sellers in the history of publishing, *The Common Sense Book of Baby and Child Care*, had been bombarding the White House with letters of protest ever since 1964, accusing President Lyndon Johnson of betraying his election promises. Early in 1968, he came out with a piece of writing that has a familiar ring for those who signed the recent petition against immigration policies in France: it was a "Call for Resistance to Illegal Authority."

Contrary to general belief, all this rebellious energy cannot – or cannot exclusively – be explained by the youth of those involved. It derived, rather, from the encounter between all those young people and the spectacular moral support they received from the great intellectuals of the day.

Following the manifesto signed by 121 signatories against France's Algerian war, Dr Spock's was the second great post-World War II call for civil disobedience. It called for illegal action to organize units of resistance to the draft and to aid resistance to the war in all appropriate ways. Among those who signed were Philip Roth, Susan Sontag, Grace Paley, Allen Ginsberg, Robert Coover, Nelson Algren, James Baldwin, Norman Mailer, William Styron and Thomas Pynchon. They undertook, again in violation of the law, to refuse to pay the 10 percent tax increase levied for the war by deducting from their own taxes the sums devoted to war. Spock and the four other promoters of the appeal (Marcus Raskin, Michael Ferber, Mitchell Goodman and the Reverend William Coffin) were prosecuted. The trial was all over the media, and the ensuing debate on the civil disobedience issue ranged the politicians (who were all anti, of course) against the artists and the intellectuals (who overwhelmingly came out in support).

Meanwhile, in many parts of the United States, draftees had already taken matters into their own hands. Back in 1966, Barry Bondus had emptied two pails of excrement over the Army's draft records. In 1967, Pastor Berrigan was sentenced to six years in jail for dousing 600 draft files with blood. In May 1968, nine Catholics — who were to become known as the Catonsville Nine — broke into the offices of their local draft board and napalmed the draft records there. A month later, in Milwaukee County, fourteen individuals went on trial for doing the same thing; the charges were burglary and arson. During that trial, the two prosecuting attorneys, Allen Sanson (a Jew) and Harold Jackson, Jr. (a Black), turned on the

administration that they served and declared the draft laws "obscene." The idea of "civil disobedience" seemed to hold no terrors for any of those who proclaimed it.

There was, of course, a price to be paid. Both in the United States and in France, police repression was so violent that in many cases it helped to radicalize the movement and make it grow. Americans were used to seeing the military called out to race riots, with all the attendant overtones of civil conflict; but nothing had prepared them for the sight of the Chicago police attacking a crowd of pacifist demonstrators led by the Yippie, Jerry Rubin. The protestors, with the active support of William Burroughs, Jean Genet and Allen Ginsberg (who answered the nightsticks and the tear gas by clashing Buddhist fingertip cymbals and chanting the Tibetan OM), asked nothing more than to be able to goof off on the corner of the street, and screw anyone at any time, plus the abolition of all laws dealing with victimless crimes (i.e., using drugs), the abolition of money and "full unemployment."

Armed with this program, the protestors poured into Chicago in August, to be met with a totally disproportionate police response. "They attacked like a saw cutting into wood," said Norman Mailer. Ranks of twenty to thirty policemen, swinging their nightsticks in an arc, maddened by the fury of their own violence. The riot squads pursued protestors, onlookers, and tourists indiscriminately, beating men, women and children until the blood flowed. They burst into the Hayward Inn restaurant through the windows and beat up everyone they found there. They also invaded the Democratic Convention, which was going on a few hundred yards away, and attacked members of the staff of one candidate, Eugene McCarthy. Mayor Richard Daley of Chicago congratulated his men and awarded them a 22 percent pay raise.

In France, the veterans of 1968 have tended to wrap their escapades in a cosy cloak of myth that has, in its turn, tended to obscure the violence of the repression that took place. One of the root causes of the French May 68 movement — some things never change — was a phenomenal increase in the number of university students; in a few years, the total had jumped from 160,000 to 514,000. The national education system could not cope. There were already proposals to reform it, by introducing a selection process for university entrance, and this infuriated the students. The first big protest came on May 6. It was a quiet affair, compared with what was happening in other countries, but it was met by a degree of police violence that ignited the powder keg. In France, during the days and nights that followed, the CRS, the french riot police, became the first force in Europe to deploy CB gas (also used in Vietnam). Not content with beating the protestors up, the CRS tossed gas grenades in through apartment windows (this at a time when much of central Paris had yet to be gentrified). "They searched the houses one by one," a witness said later. "Anyone who had hands blackened or clothes stained by the gas was beaten up and arrested."

A nurse, who came in to tend the wounded and found herself arrested, later told what she had seen at the detention center: "The CRS buses disgorged men and women who had been beaten or gassed, with head wounds, broken arms, etc. The Chinese and Vietnamese, and especially the Blacks, had been treated with particular brutality… One young man came past me, half naked, with his legs lacerated by blows from billy clubs; he was bleeding, holding his belly, and pissing everywhere. A young woman, who had been with him, told me that the CRS had clubbed him unconscious, stripped him, and then beaten him on the genitalia until the skin was hanging off him in tatters."

It was a violent time. In Mexico City, a few weeks before the Olympic Games were due to open, the army opened fire on a crowd, killing or injuring several hundred people. In Germany, 120 people were injured in a demonstration against the Springer publishing group. Fourteen were killed in Milan by a bomb laid – the first of many – by persons unknown. In Poland, under pressure from a governmental campaign of anti-Semitism, 2,000 Jews left the country during the year. In Japan, in October, over 800 people were injured in riots. In the United States, clashes between students, Blacks and police were endemic.

It must be said that a lot of the violence was verbal. What strikes us now, in reading the declarations of that time, is the gap between what was actually happening in people's experience and the perception of it by the student ideologues. Rather than analyze American racism, for example, the Black Panthers, then as later, fell back on anti-Semitic rhetoric. The Jews, proclaimed a poem published in the magazine *Black Power*, had stolen the Blacks' bread, their bitch women had enticed the men into their beds, and they must be exterminated.

In France, Maoist leaders entrenched themselves in an ideology that had no contact whatsoever with the real world – either in China or in France. This lack of connection was probably responsible for the students' inability to forge an alliance with labor. Since one side was hog-tied by ideological preconceptions, and the other was kept on a short rein by a hostile Communist Party, chances of unity were slim indeed.

The views of the historian Staughton Lynd provide a good definition of the aspirations of the time – and one that now seems oddly contemporary. So long as the revolution was described to him in terms of a violent insurrection, it seemed both unpleasant and unreal; and the

The Russians were reduced to firing on children (a twelve-year-old was shot on Wenceslas Square, while trying to insert a Czech flag in the gun barrel of a Russian tank) and on women. They patrolled the streets with eyes downcast in shame; some of them wept.

traditional alternative, that of Social Democracy, whereby the Left would take power peacefully in a succession of elections, appeared equally illusory.

The thing to do was to attack the system one bit at a time, using the strategy of nonviolent, direct action. This was the principle of civil disobedience, which in some cases extended to the creation of counter-institutions. But the sterile, jargon-ridden utterances of the militants – whether Maoist, Trotskyist, Guevarist, or whatever – contributed at least as much as police repression did to the destruction of that initial impetus. The Vietnam War, and more generally the emergence of Third World issues, led most of the militant leaders to make virtual nonsense of their own positions – to the point of adopting entirely contradictory attitudes. Under a cloak of dialectics, the advancement of libertarian Socialism went hand in hand with the glorification of dictators, whether Vietnamese, Chinese or Russian (via Cuba). Most of the older intellectuals, who had wrested their own freedom of thought from Stalinist Communism ten or twenty years before, were not prepared to listen to the American student leader, Tom Hayden, justifying the Russian occupation of Prague on the grounds that there might be some counterrevolutionaries among the Czechs.

In all likelihood, events in Prague were the closest thing anywhere in the world to the true "civil disobedience" that was so much sought after in the West. After the tanks moved in, on the night of August 21-22, the population spontaneously set up a movement of "passive resistance." The Russians tore down the posters and slogans calling for them to go home but, the next day, there they were back on the walls. On the night of August 23, all of the street names were torn down and replaced with the one name of Dubcek, the man who had presided over the "Prague Spring" that Moscow was determined to crush. The Russians were reduced to

firing on children (a twelve-year-old was shot on Wenceslas Square, while trying to insert a Czech flag in the gun barrel of a Russian tank) and on women. They patrolled the streets with eyes downcast in shame; some of them wept.

In the West, confronted by their own ideological contradictions and by an increasingly brutal campaign of repression, student leaders increasingly entrenched themselves in arid rhetoric. Irving Horowitz, though himself one of the theoreticians of the New Left, pointed out that Fascism was making a comeback, virtually as a leftwing ideology. Anyone who remembered the Nazis' use of the term Saujuden, Jew swine, ought to reflect on the implications of using the word "pig" – the very same word that Jerry Rubin's Yippies applied indiscriminately to all defenders of the System. Horowitz had a point. Not long afterward, Charles Manson – the idol of the leftist Weathermen – was denouncing the "pigs" in the same way when he murdered Sharon Tate.

Three decades later, it is difficult to think oneself back into the mindset of 1968. Modernity is no longer modern; the young are no longer young; the objects around us have turned out to be more of a menace than anyone could have believed – not to mention what has happened to the denunciation of the consumer society in a world ravaged by unemployment; and to sexual freedom in the age of AIDS; to communications; to postcolonial society. The enthusiasm that was once directed toward Cuba and the role model of Che Guevara now tends to be channeled into merchandising; and the Biafran massacres, which so appalled public opinion in 1968 that they gave rise to many individual vocations (notably those of the "French Doctors," Médecins sans Frontières), have now become hideously routine – in Rwanda, in

What remains of 1968, therefore, is not so much the answers that were proclaimed with such certainty but the questions, many of which still present themselves in precisely the same terms: the plight of the Third World, the race issue in the United States, the future of the French education system — and the necessity for civil disobedience, which has been quite recently rediscovered in France.

Somalia and tomorrow, undoubtedly, somewhere else. Now that the Wall has fallen, the Russian tanks in Prague look like ancient history; though they can also be seen as the first sign of the growing chaos that now afflicts the countries of Eastern Europe. As for the attraction of Hinduism and of Oriental philosophies, it has given way to the New Age in all its forms, and to a vast range of panaceas. Marshall Applewhite, the guru of the Heaven's Gate sect in the United States, who led 39 of his followers in a mass suicide early in 1997, had taught music on the campuses of the 1960s.

People in 1968 were subject to a number of optical illusions that we can now see for what they were. On April 23 the students of Columbia University, New York, one of the most respected Ivy League schools, took over their campus and unleashed one of the toughest student revolts of the year. On the very same day, by an extraordinary coincidence, an apparently similar rising took place at Tsinghua University in the northeastern suburbs of Beijing. Of course, this happenstance was exploited, notably by the Maoists, as the sign of an international upsurge of revolutionary fervor among the young. We now know that, in reality, the two were very different. Where the Columbia students were demonstrating for an end to the Vietnam War (and for the right to attend classes in tracksuits), those who killed each other with submachine guns in the courtyard at Tsinghua were two factions of Red Guards, and they were doing it for the greater glory of Chairman Mao. When the Chinese university eventually reopened its doors, the department of sociology — that discipline so popular among the Western rebels — was closed for good.

What remains of 1968, therefore, is not so much the answers that were proclaimed with such certainty but the questions, many of which still present themselves in precisely the same terms: the plight of the Third World, the race issue in the United States, the future of the French education system — and the necessity for civil disobedience, which has been quite recently rediscovered in France.

Another thing that endures — and perhaps this is the most positive legacy of 1968 — is the memory of the astonishing self-assurance of it all, the rebellious courage that stopped at nothing. After the upheavals of Chicago in August 1968, Jerry Rubin and Abbie Hoffman, the leaders of the Yippie movement, were summoned to appear before the Un-American Activities Committee. Rubin showed up wearing a Black Panther beret, with Indian war-paint on his face and a Mexican bandolier (full of live shells) across his bare chest. Hoffman made his entrance in a judge's robe; he was told to take it off, and did so, only to reveal that he was defiantly wearing a policeman's shirt underneath. At the same hearings, Ginsberg, called as a defense witness, started reciting his own poem *Howl!* while pointing a finger at the judge with a Messianic gesture: "Moloch the vast stone of war! Moloch whose blood is running money!"

Whereupon the trial turned into a fist-fight, and the defense attorney, William Kunstler, fell on his knees and begged to be arrested.

It is true that Rubin and Hoffman elsewhere proclaimed some eccentric political views, that they regarded Charles Manson as a "poetic personality" whose "courage" was an inspiration to them, and that Random House brought out Hoffman's book with a publicity campaign that presented every potential reader as a conspirator, thus giving a pleasurable frisson of excitement to the bourgeoisie: all this is true, and now seems somewhat pathetic. But it counts for less than the underlying attitude itself, the sense that absolutely anything was possible. "Any view of the world that is not bizarre is false," said one of the lesser-known graffiti slogans of the May 68 rising in Paris.

The music of that time still carries the same fearsome charge of energy. "When you got nothing / You got nothing to lose," sings Dylan; and Janis Joplin seems to answer him with "Freedom is just another word for nothing else to lose." A world away from the ideological slogans of that period, these are the words I shall remember. I still cherish 1968 for its elegant exaltation, for its laid-back lyricism, and for a near-suicidal hope that expected nothing of life but life itself.

The March on the Pentagon,
anti-Vietnam war protest,
Washington, D.C., October 1967.
Marc Riboud.

The crowd then set off toward the Pentagon, the vast building of the Defense Department, where the second half of Saturday's demonstration was scheduled to take place. The government had organized an enormous military and police presence here, the biggest ever seen in the capital: 6,000 soldiers and military police were waiting with fixed bayonets. There was an equal number of civil police, all in helmets and holding nightsticks. Other forces were held in reserve in the Washington area. The whole police operation was under the command of General Throckmorton, who last summer commanded the Federal troops sent to tame the rioting Blacks in Detroit.

¡VENCEREMOS!

CHE VIVE DONDE LOS PUEBLOS LUCHA
MPI

RE NEW NAZIS
TO DEFEAT THEM
EPENDENCE

March on the Pentagon, Washington, D.C., October 1967. Che Guevara had died ten days previously.
Marc Riboud.

About twenty demonstrators, including several young women, managed to find their way inside the forbidden walls of the Pentagon. Soldiers used rifle-butts to force them back, and those that fell were trampled underfoot. That evening, witnesses reported seeing pools of blood where the charge took place. Large numbers of demonstrators were injured by blows from police nightsticks, the civil police seeming even more eager than the military to use their weapons. The police used tear gas, though this was denied by the authorities, who had the effrontery to suggest that the demonstrators themselves had seized the tear gas grenades and thrown them into the crowd.

L'Humanité, October 23, 1967

Anti-Vietnam war protest,
Central Park, New York.
The sign shows a caricature of
President Lyndon Johnson.
Burt Glinn

March on the Pentagon,
Washington,D.C., October 1967. *Marc Riboud.*

As darkness fell, the demonstrators settled down to what some said would be an all-night vigil. However, at midnight, United States marshals began systematically picking up demonstrators encamped at the east entrance of the Mall steps and carrying them to waiting vans. At that point it was estimated that the troops outnumbered the demonstrators on the Mall who had dwindled to about 1,000.

Joseph A. Lofters,
The New York Times,
October 22, 1967

MANKIND MUST PUT
AN END TO WAR, OR
AN END

On Monday night, the NLF
(National Liberation Front)
launched violent surprise
attacks on U.S. bases and
on the towns of Da-Nang,
Nha-Trang, Qui-Nhon, Kontun,
Pleiku, Ban-Me-Thuot and
Tan-Canh. The only centers
of population spared in South
Vietnam that night were the
Mekong Delta towns and the
capital, Saigon. In Saigon a
state of alert was declared,
and authorities expected
suicide bombings of U.S. and
South Vietnamese military
installations.

Le Monde, January 31

Tet offensive: Vietnamese
civilians flee American bombing.
Saigon, January-February.
Philip Jones-Griffiths

Tet offensive, Saigon,
January-February.
Philip Jones-Griffiths.

21

et offensive, Saigon, January-February.
hilip Jones-Griffiths.

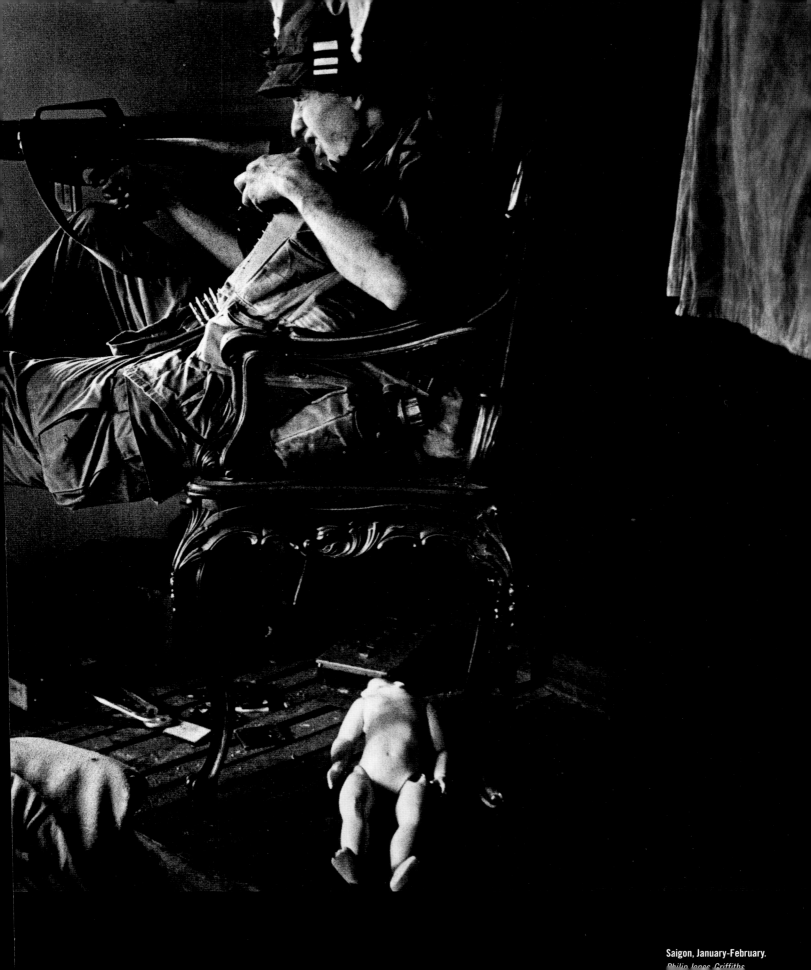

Saigon, January-February.
Philip Jones Griffiths

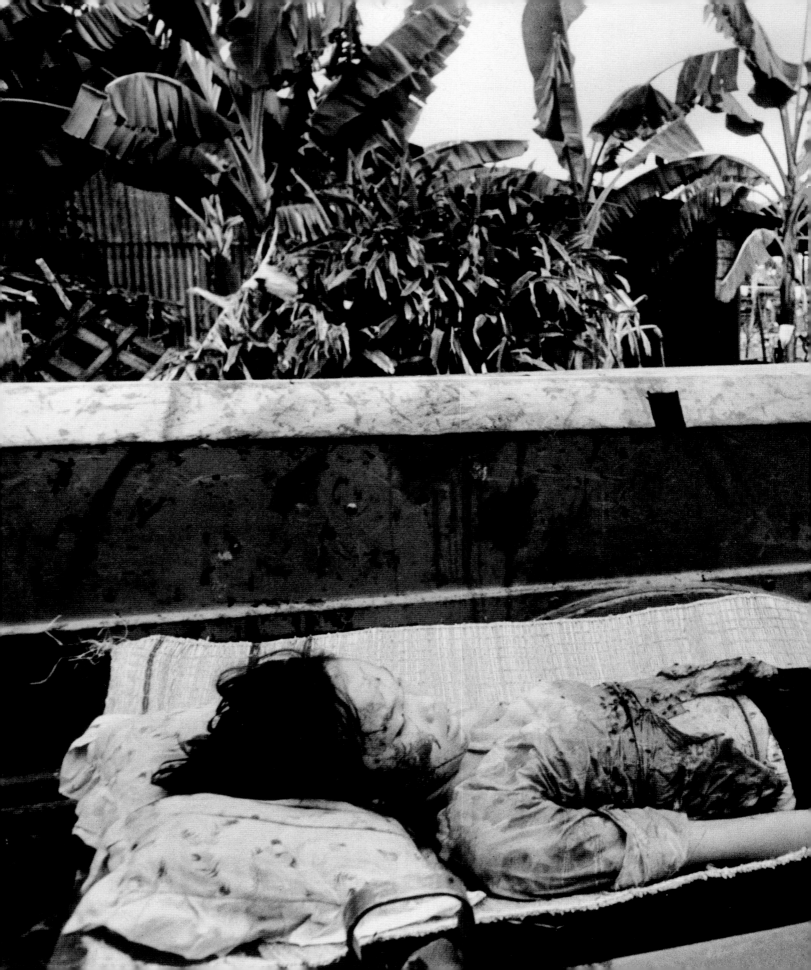

Tet offensive: a boy weeps for
his sister, killed by a round
fired from an American helicopter.
Near Saigon, January-February.
Philip Jones Griffiths

Internally, the Vietcong have won an important victory. They have demonstrated to the Vietnamese their ability to strike where and when they choose. They have held up the Saigon government and their army to ridicule. To the discomfiture of Saigon, they have tightened their hold on the civilian population, which may not be sympathetic to them but is now filled with respect, fear and admiration.

Max Clos, *Le Figaro,* January 31

The Pentagon is putting a brave face on things. Staff have received strict instructions to avoid defeatist talk.

J. Jacquet-Francillon, *Le Figaro,* February

Bomb crater in the area where the American Air Force attempted to cut the Ho Chi Minh Trail.
Philip Jones-Griffiths

We must develop a true
proletarian internationalism,
with international proletarian
armies, for whom the flag
beneath which they fight
becomes the sacred cause
of the redemption of humanity.
To die beneath the colors
of Vietnam, Venezuela,
Guatemala, Laos, Guinea,
Colombia, Bolivia, Brazil
– to name only the current
theaters of armed struggle –
should be equally glorious
and desirable for an American,
an Asian, an African, even
a European.

Ernesto Che Guevara, *Writings of a
Revolutionary*

Cuban artist 's installation during the
Cultural Congress in Havana, January.
d Mayer.

Silhouettes of Che Guevara,
Camilo Cienfuegos
and Fidel Castro, Cuba.
Fred Mayer.

3

NAM: LECCION PARA EL MUNDO

New Year's parade, Havana.
Sugarcane workers are seen saluting
Vietnamese freedom fighters. *Fred Mayer.*

Red Guards on parade, Beijing. *Marc Riboud.*

Schoolchildren training
for a Havana street parade during
the Cuban Cultural Congress. *Fred Mayer.*

Demonstration in Beijing against the

Poverty stricken district
of New Orleans.
Abbas.

With another plea against violence and for the legal redress of injustice, President Johnson signed today the Civil Rights Act of 1968. Its major provision is intended to end racial discrimination in the sale and rental of 80 percent of the nation's homes and apartments. [...] The President displayed the pride that comes, he said, with the signing of the "promises of a century." Few thought when he proposed it at a White House meeting two years ago that fair housing would "in our time" become the law of the land, he said, "and now at long last this afternoon its day has come." [...] "There is much to do," the President said, and after his program is enacted there will be still more to do.

The New York Times, April 12

This page:
"Black is beautiful." The first mass manufactured black dolls, Harlem, New York.
Eve Arnold.

Right hand page:
Fanny Lou Hammer, civil rights campaigner, visits a Southern family.
Bruce Davidson.

42

Now we are engaged in a psychological struggle in this country and that struggle is whether or not black people have the right to use the words they want to use without white people giving their sanction to it. We maintain, whether they like it or not, we gon' use the word "black power" and let them address themselves to that. We are not gonna wait for white people to sanction black power. We're tired of waiting. Every time black people move in this country, they're forced to defend their position before they move. It's time that the people who're supposed to be defending their position do that. That's white people. They ought to start defending them- selves, as to why they have oppressed and exploited us.

Stokely Carmichael, *"Black Power,"* speech given November 19, 1966, at the University of California, Berkeley

Harlem.
Abbas

Above left: **The Rev. Dr. Martin Luther King, Jr.,** speaking
outside the United Nations in New York. *Burt Glinn.*
Above right: **James Baldwin.** *Guy Le Querrec.*
Below left: **James Brown** interviewed after a concert in Harlem. The slogan
"Black is beautiful" was launched by him on this occasion. *Eve Arnold.*
Below right: **Black Power leader Stokely Carmichael.** *Burt Glinn.*

A 16 year-old Negro youth was killed today in violence surrounding a massive protest march that was led through downtown Memphis by the Rev. Dr. Martin Luther King, Jr. A group of Negro youths smashed windows and looted stores as Dr. King led 6, 000 demonstrators in support of the city's striking sanitation workers, most of them Negroes. Local leaders of the march halted the procession as the disorders continued.
As the march turned back the police began using tear gas and chemical mace, an irritant, to clear the streets.

Walter Rugaber, *The New York Times,*
March 29

The Poor People's March,
Washington, D.C., March.
Constantine Manos.

Marchers at the Capitol,
Washington, D.C., March.
Constantine Manos.

49

1. We want freedom. We want power to determine the destiny of our Black Community.

2. We want full employment for our people.

3. We want an end to the robbery by the white man of our Black Community.

4. We want decent housing, fit for shelter of human beings.

5. We want education for our people that exposes the true nature of this decadent American society. We want education that teaches us our true history and our role in the present-day society.

6. We want all black men to be exempt from military service.

7. We want an immediate end to police brutality and murder of black people.

8. We want freedom for all black men held in federal, state, county and city prisons and jails.

9. We want all black people when brought to trial to be tried in court by a jury of their peer group or people from their black communities, as defined by the Constitution of the United States.

A member of the Black Panthers addressing students in Chicago.
Hiroji Kubota.

The attempt on his [Rudi Dutschke's] life unleashed a strong wave of feeling all over the Federal Republic of Germany [...] The German League of Socialist Students (SDS), to which Rudi Dutschke belonged, described it as the outcome of the propaganda campaign waged by the Springer press and on Thursday evening organized a demonstration outside the group's Berlin offices. Several thousand demonstrators brandishing torches tried to storm Springer House; they broke through a light cordon of police and managed to make their way into the garage, where they set fire to about fifteen vehicles. By 1 a.m. on Friday, the police had the upper hand. Many were injured on both sides.

Le Monde, April 13

The East and the West are organizing more and more, at the expense of the underdeveloped countries. Today the oppressed have only one option, that of armed struggle. For them, the future means Revolution. How much longer will we allow the killing to go on in our name? AMERICANS OUT OF VIETNAM!

Rudi Dutschke,
International Front for Freedom

Street scene in Germany.

Rudi Dutschke, leader of the SDS
(League of German Socialist Students).
The April 11 attempt on his life sparked off
violent demonstrations all over Germany. *Thomas Hoepker*

The problem is this: there is a seemingly unbridgeable gulf between an older generation who rebuilt Germany economically, but who have lost their moral credibility, and the young people who know of a nation's hardships and suffering only by hearsay, and who seek a new morality through ideological commitment.

So they confront each other with no mutual understanding: the older generation, most of whom stood in line to swear the oath of loyalty to Hitler, and the young who, for the sake of a better world, start fires and toss paving stones; the old who, with the Grand Coalition, have made a travesty of parliamentary politics, and the young who want to create a new democracy by extraparliamentary means; the old who deny their principles out of sheer pragmatism and the young who, because they are so crammed with principles, seem incapable of defining an objective.

Der Spiegel, April 22

Vietnam war protest
in the Ruhr, Germany.
Leonard Freed

Below the conservative working classes there is a whole substratum of pariahs and outsiders, people of other races, other skin colors, the exploited and the persecuted, the unemployed and the unemployable. These people exist outside the democratic process; their lives illustrate the urgent, inescapable need to put an end to institutions and conditions that are intolerable. Their opposition is revolutionary, even if their consciousness is not.

Herbert Marcuse,
One-Dimensional Man, 1964

Herbert Marcuse.
Marc Riboud.

Top: **Karl Jaspers with his wife.** *Thomas Hoepker.*
Bottom left: **Günter Grass.** *Herbert List.*
Bottom right: **Milos Forman.** *David Hurn.*

Top left: **Carnival in Slovakia.**
Top right: **Election of Miss Student in Moravia, May.**
Bottom left: **The Wind Festival, Moravia, May.**
Bottom right: **Student festival, Moravia, May.**
Josef Koudelka.

**Believe in thought
reason
man as he really is
socialist democracy
intelligence
paradox
chance
liberty
yourself
Do not believe in
ideology
the faceless masses
power
totalitarian dictatorship
certainty
plans
necessity
authority
Young people, believe in
yourselves.**

Ivan Svitak, extracts from *Your Head Against the Wall*, an essay dedicated to the students of the faculty of letters at Charles University, Prague, published in *Student*, no. 6, spring, 1968.

May Day parade, Prague.
Josef Koudelka.

Alexander Dubcek, Antonin Novotny and Walter
Ulbricht celebrating the 20th anniversary of
the Communist coup of February 1948.
Josef Koudelka.

Student demonstration
during the presidential
election campaign.
Josef Koudelka.

Presidential election,
parade in Prague Castle.
Josef Koudelka.

Anniversary of the Communist
coup of 1948. People's Militia
in the old city, Prague.
Josef Koudelka.

We needed to encourage this country to accept new principles, new ways of thinking about mental illnesses. We could do this only by bringing forward a new law to allow, for example, a mental patient to appear against the hospital-ization that has been forced upon him. We had to give special guarantees to citizens who had lost their democratic rights. And, when they leave the psychiatric hospital, we had to find a way to provide them with another guarantee: that the patient will not be hounded for the rest of his life by a police record of time spent in the institution.

Mariotti, Italian minister of health
in Franco Perini, "Se il matto
è un uomo" [Is a Lunatic
a Human Being?],
L'Europeo

Carnival at the psychiatric hospital
in Udine, Italy, February.
Ferdinando Scianna.

In 1968, in the psychiatric hospital
of which he was the director,
Franco Basaglio raised the
question of the confinement and
treatment of mental patients in
Western society. The result was a
debate over the true nature of our
culture and civilization that still
continues to this day. It was one of
the most significant outcomes of
the 1968 phenomenon.

Their discussions are held in community groups. We spent two days in Gorizia and heard speeches by both women and men; they discussed matters of concern to them, such as why Ward D had not been on an outing for a long time, why the women in the dressmaking shop opposed the transfer of the dining room to their workroom, why it was pointless to worry every time there was a grass snake in the park: "Signora Giovanna spoke with a lady who works in the fields; she said she had seen a grass snake, but a grass snake is not venomous."

It would be wrong, very wrong, to report that these men and women talk like us and can argue like us. They do it better. Their way of discussing things, their dialectic of opposing views, their skill in reaching conclusions without scapegoating or making anyone feel defeated, is superior to ours.

Franco Perini, "Se il matto è un uomo" [Is a Lunatic a Human Being?], *L'Europeo*

Psychiatric hospital in Gorizia, Italy. *Ferdinando Scianna*

**Students occupying the Liceo
(high school), Parma, Italy.** *Ferdinando Scianna.*
Student protest Milan, Italy. *Ferdinando Scianna.*

The young were products of urbanization, and of the consumer society that had "corrupted" their parents' moral and civic values and replaced them with materialism. We should applaud the present renewal of interest in politics: despite the risks attendant on immaturity, the explosion of protest among the young is an extremely positive development. The eagerness to argue politics, to debate society, and to hero-worship Third World revolutionary leaders from Guevara to Mao, stems from a moral need and from the desire for a fairer society. The leaders who are now chairing meetings or heading up movements have in common this moralizing insistence on purity.

Giovanni Russo,
"Le voci nuove della democrazia,"
Il Corriere della sera, December 31

Student protest, Milan, Italy.
Ferdinando Scianna.

Street arrests

IF YOU ARE ARRESTED

1. Remain calm.

2. Have the telephone number of the October 27th Legal Defence Committee with you at all times. It is 734-4827.

3. Take the number of the cop who ACTUALLY arrests you. This is VERY IMPORTANT as you will later be "assigned" an "arresting officer" who you may never have seen before who will testify to your guilt.

4. DON'T TALK TO THE COPS. Make no statement of any kind. Give your correct name and address. [...]

10. IN COURT demand to be represented by an OLD lawyer, but if one is not available, a lawyer appointed by the court is better than nothing. Make sure the lawyer knows your background history which is important when setting bail for postponed hearings.

Advice for the demonstration against the Vietnam war in Grosvenor Square, *The Black Dwarf*, July 13.

Anti-Vietnam war protest, London, March 17.
David Hurn.

Anti-Vietnam war protest,
London, March 17.
David Hurn

74

I remember many wars.
I can recall nothing in my
experience to compare
with the situation
[in Vietnam]. I can
find in my memory no
example of a people so
tortured and yet
so utterly devoid of the
vices of their tormentor.
I can think of no conflic
in which the disparity of
strength between the tw
sides is so great.

Bertrand Russell

Bertrand Russell, who in 1966
set up the tribunal that bore
his name to hear evidence
of U.S. war crimes in Vietnam.
David Hurn

Anti-Vietnam war protest,
Grosvenor Square,
London, July 7.

MEDICAL AID DEFENCE

Because it is never certain to
what lengths the cops may go
when "controlling" a crowd, w
have medical aid people read
to help you if you have been
attacked and can't get other
medical help at once.

We must be ready. This time
the police may use tear gas to
attack the crowd. This is what
to do :

1. Take short even breaths. Do
not gulp as the gas will only g
deeper into the lungs.

2. If gas gets in your eyes, ON
NO ACCOUNT RUB THEM.

3. If you have been gassed, YO
MUST NOT DRINK FOR THREE
HOURS although you may feel
very thirsty. Stay cool.

Advice for the demonstration
against the Vietnam war in Grosvenor
Square, *The Black Dwarf*, July 13.

Mounted police charge in Grosvenor
Square, in front of U.S. embassy,
London, March 17.
David Hurn

Everywhere I hear the
sound of marching,
charging feet boy
'Cause summers have end
the time is right for
fighting in the street boy

[Chorus]
So what can a poor boy do
except to sing
For a rockn'roll band
'cause in sleepy London
town there's no place for
a Street Fighting Man

They said the time is right
for a palace revolution
But where I live the game
to play is compromise
solution

They said my name is
called disturbance
I'll shout and scream
I'll kill the king
I'll rail at all his servants

Street Fighting Man, unpublished
Rolling Stones song that English
record producers refused to release.
Mick Jagger gave it to the magazine
The Black Dwarf, who reproduced it
in their October issue .

Anti-Vietnam war protest,
Grosvenor Square,
London, March 17.

Student leader Tariq Ali
and actress Vanessa Redgrave
lead anti-Vietnam war protest,
London, March 17.
David Hurn.

Children during
the Biafran war.
Don McCullin.

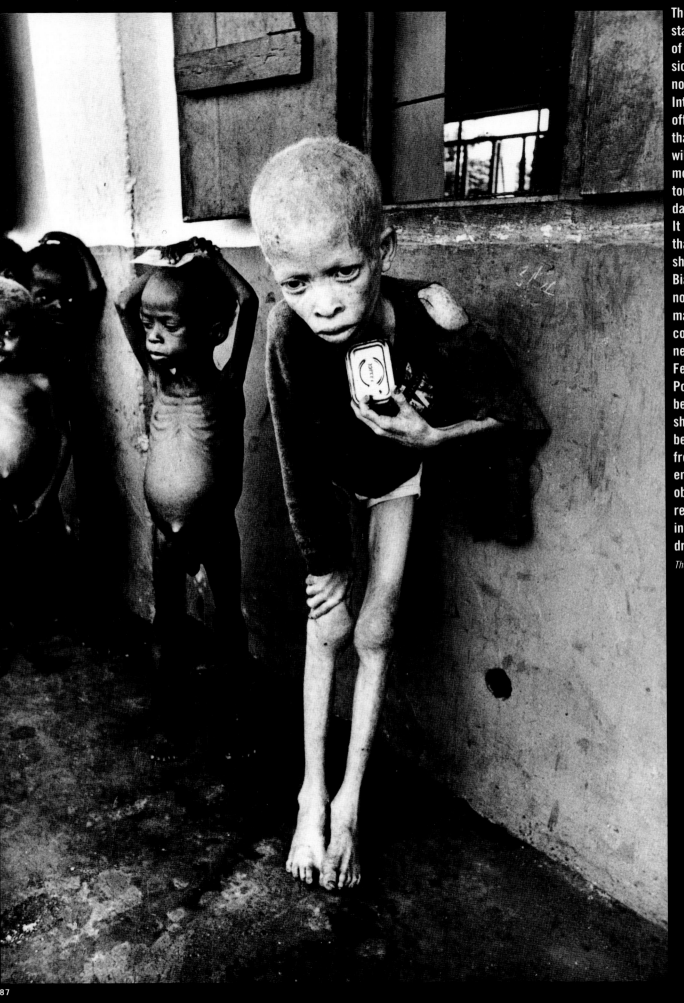

The awful dimensions of starvation in what is left of the Nigerian secessionist state of Biafra are now starkly evident. An International Red Cross official says that more than a million Biafrans will die of hunger within a month unless at least 200 tons of food can be sent daily into the area. [...] It is probable, however, that only overland food shipments can cope with Biafra's needs. Biafra now has only one or two makeshift airfields which could not handle the necessary food traffic. Federal officials say Port Harcourt cannot be opened for normal shipping for months because the channel from Bonny has not been entirely cleared of obstacles left by the retreating Biafrans, and in any case must be dredged.

The New York Times, July 5

The ruins of Hue, the former imperial capital of Vietnam, after bombing by the Americans, February. *Marc Riboud.*

An area of hundreds of square feet has been completely flattened by aerial bombing and rocket fire. Nearby, six armored vehicles, two of them tanks, are still burning, having been hit by Vietcong rockets. During Tuesday's violent clashes, the Vietcong used a rickshaw to transport a large recoilless 75 millimeter weapon. When spotted by the Americans, they hurriedly unhooked the gun and vanished into a warren of houses.

Le Figaro, February 2

On the bridge destroyed by the Vietcong to block the U.S. Marines offensive against the citadel of Hue, the inhabitants are attempting to flee the city. February.
Philip Jones-Griffiths

The "interrogation" of a
Vietnamese civilian
by U.S. Marines.
Don McCullie

[...] At nightfall, the Marines held only two square blocks of the smoking city. And seven South Vietnamese Army battalions struggled unsucessfully to push North Vietnamese and Vietcong troops from the Citadel. [...]
The strength of the enemy resistance caught the South Vietnamese by surprise. [...]
The New York Times, February 3

One of the wounded is evacuated.
Don McCullin.

5

[...] In breaking through Hue the marines suffered 10 dead, and 20 to 30 wounded. They reported that they had killed 50 Vietcong and wounded many others.
The South Vietnamese Army estimated that it had killed 200 enemy soldiers and described its own losses as light. [...] The two allied forces are working separately rather than as a coordinated unit.

The New York Times, February 3

An American clergyman helping an old Vietnamese woman to escape from the combat zone.
Don McCullin

The body of a North Vietnamese. American soldiers

Peace demonstrator, Santa Monica. "Waste more land" alludes to the name of the U.S. Commander-in-Chief in Vietnam, General Westmoreland.
Dennis Stock.

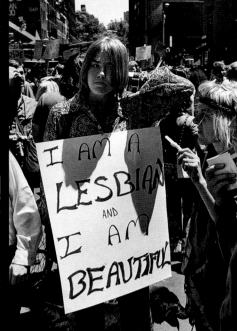

Demonstrations in favor of the legalization of abortion
and the decriminalization of homosexuality, New York.
Elliott Landy (above left) and Leonard Freed

Rock festival at Venice
Beach, California.
Dennis Stock.

103

"Love is free": hippie movements and communities in California.
Dennis Stock (above) and Roger Malloch

Hippies in California
Dennis Stock

Above left: **Jerry Rubin and Abbie Hoffman at a Black Panther gathering in New Haven, Connecticut.** *Leonard Freed.*
Above right: **Demonstration against the Vietnam war at the Democratic Convention, young man burning his draft card.**
Below: **A member of the Yippie movement (Youth International Party).**

Some call us Hippies or Yippies or marginals or dropouts or free men or flower children. The name is not important. For the time being, here we are. We are waging our own War of Secession… With our long hair, we are the new Negroes. It marks us out. It symbolizes our rejection of the old order… army, career, college crap, outdated conventions, open-plan apartment…
Abbie Hoffman

The ideological left is made up of part-time revolutionaries whose lifestyle belies their words.
Jerry Rubin

Militant selling the Free Press, one of the many alternative newspapers and magazines launched at this time. Sunset Boulevard, Los Angeles.
Dennis Stock

Biker gang, Colorado. *Dennis Stock.*

The Rev. Dr. Martin Luther
King, Jr. who preached
non-violence and racial
brotherhood, was fatally
shot here last night by a
distant gunman who then
raced away and escaped.
[...]
A curfew was imposed
on the shocked city of
550,000 inhabitants, 40
percent of whom are
Negro.
But the police said
the tragedy had been
followed by incidents
that included sporadic
shooting, fires, bricks
and bottles thrown at
policemen, and looting
that started in Negro
districts and then spread
over the city.

The New York Times, April 5

Announcement on American television of the assassination
of Martin Luther King, April 5. *René Burri.*

Washington, April 5 (Special) — The National Guard was ordered into five states today following the assassination of the Rev. Martin Luther King, Jr., and federal troops were sent into Washington to maintain law and order in the face of widespread Negro rioting.
[...]
The violence started last night as the first shock waves from Dr. King's murder rolled through the country's ghettos. It continued today with schools being closed, turning bands of enraged youths free on the streets to riot and loot.

International Herald Tribune, April 6-7

The National Guard is brought in to control rioting after the assassination of Martin Luther King, Washington, D.C., April 6.
Burt Glinn.

The day after the riots that followed the assassination
of Martin Luther King, Washington, D.C., April 7. *Burt Glinn.*

Coretta Scott King and her children beside her husband's coffin, Atlanta, April 9.
Constantine Manos.

**March for "The King," Central Park,
New York, April 9.** *Bruce Davidson.*

Senator Eugene MacCarthy at the funeral of Martin Luther King,
Atlanta, April 9. *Constantine Manos.*

Robin
1927 CHES

**Robert Kennedy
on the campaign trail,
Philadelphia, March-April**
Burt Glinn

123

Senator Robert F. Kennedy has decided to become a candidate for the Democratic Presidential nomination.

The Senator scheduled a news conference for 10 A.M. today in Washington. Close friends said he would announce his candidacy then. [...]

The Senator's news conference today will be in the Caucus Room of the Old Senate Office Building. This is the room where his brother, John F. Kennedy, announced his candidacy for the Presidency in 1960. John Kennedy was 42 years old then. Robert Kennedy is 42 now.

Richard Witkin, *The New York Times*, March 16

Robert Kennedy on his airplane (above) during the electoral campaign, March-April.
Burt Glinn.

The day after the announcement of his candidature for the Presidency, Robert Kennedy works at home with his team. Right, his brother Ted; center, leaning forward, his secretary Kenny O'Donnell; back to camera, Ted Sorenson. Virginia, March 17.
Burt Glinn.

"I have a short announcement to read which I will read at this time. Senator Robert Francis Kennedy died at 1:44 A.M. today, June 6, 1968. With Senator Kennedy at the time of his death was his wife, Ethel; his sisters, Mrs. Patricia Lawford and Mrs. Stephen Smith; his brother-in-law, Stephen Smith, and his sister-in-law, Mrs. John F. Kennedy. He was 42 years old."
Frank Mankiewicz,
Kennedy's campaign spokesman,
as quoted in *The New York Times*, June 6

Americans pay tribute to Robert Kennedy along the route of the train taking his body from New York to Washington. New Jersey, June 7.
Burt Glinn.

Jackie Kennedy and her sister-in-law at the funeral
of Robert Kennedy, Washington, D.C., June 8. *Constantine Manos.*

Robert Kennedy's funeral,
Arlington National Cemetery,
Washington, D.C., June 8.
Fred Mayer.

By fall of '68 the mini
look was finished. The
year had started off with
crotch-high hemlines,
but by spring you saw all
different length skirts on
the fashionable people.
And with all the new
talk about above-the
knee/midcalf/to-the-
floor/wherever, women
were wearing more pants
suits. This was the season
of the great debates
about which of the best
restaurants would let a
lady in with pants on.
There were big contro-
versies and interviews
with all the maître d's.

Andy Warhol, *POPism*, 1980

Andy Warhol's reflection
in one of his celebrated
Campbell's soup cans.
Philippe Halsman.

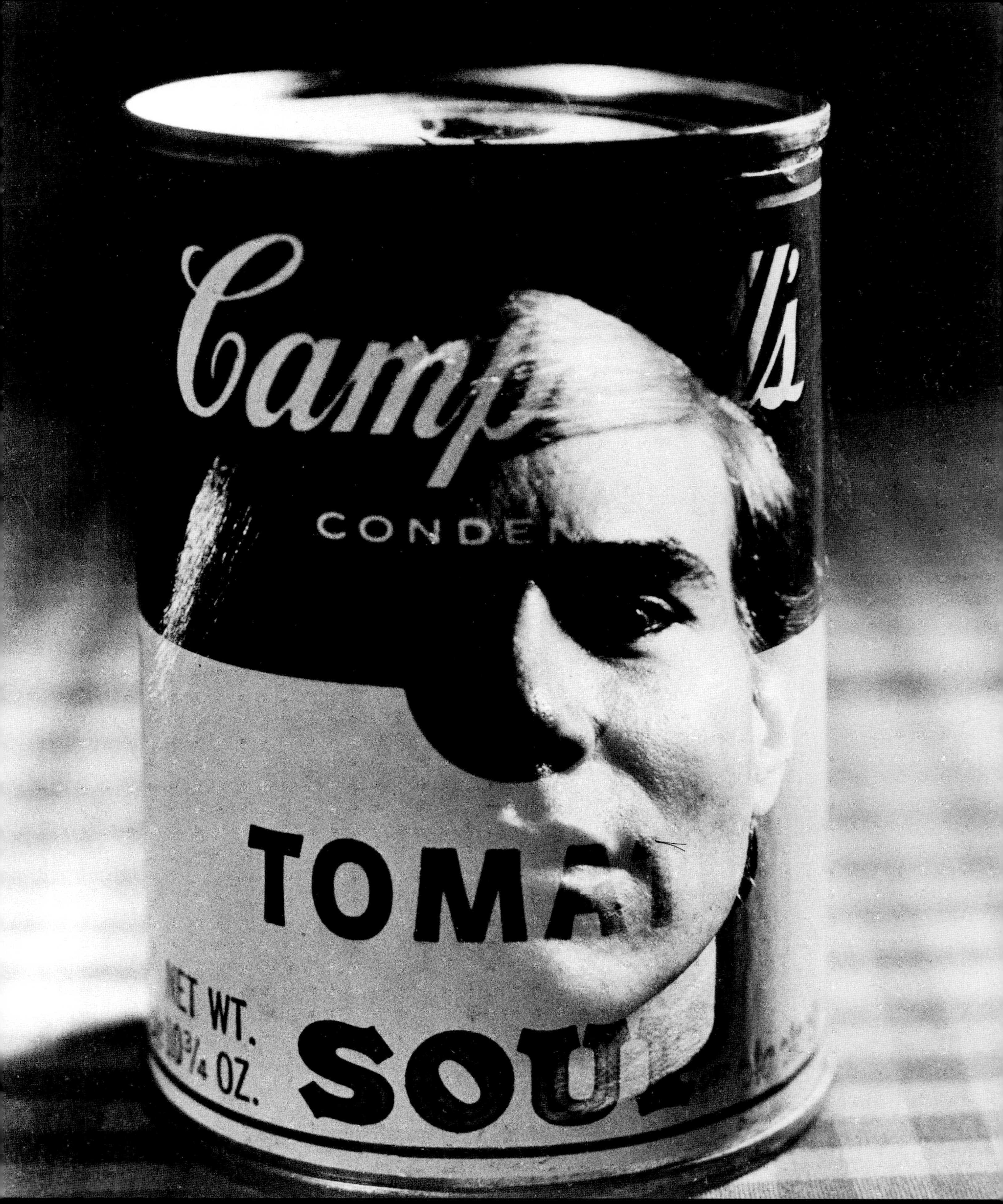
Campb
CONDE
TOMA
NET WT.
10¾ OZ.
SOU

Janis Joplin is hooked. She has to turn on almost every night. "I'm on an audience trip," she says. "When I go onstage to sing, it's like the "rush" that people experience when they take heavy dope. I talk to the audience, look into their eyes. I need them and they need me. Sex is the closest I can come to explaining it, but it's more than sex. I get stoned from happiness. I want to do it until it isn't there any more." [...] Last week at the Newport Folk Festival, a crowd of 17,800 clapped and roared for encores until nearly 1 a.m.
Time Magazine, August 9

Janis Joplin during a concert in New York State.
Elliott Landy.

Top left: **Bob Dylan**. *Elliott Landy.*
Top right: **Joan Baez at the Newport Folk Festival**. *Elliott Landy.*
Bottom left: **Jimi Hendrix on stage at the Fillmore East, New York**. *Elliott Landy.*

He [Jimi Hendrix] slung the guitar low over swivelling hips, or raised it to pick the strings with his teeth; he thrust it between his legs and did a bump and grind, crooning: "Oh, baby, come on now, sock it to me!" Lest anybody miss his message, he looked at a girl in the front row, cried, "I want you, you, you!" and stuck his tongue out at her. For a symbolic finish, he lifted the guitar and flung it against the amplifiers.

Account of a Jimi Hendrix concert at the Public Music Hall in Cleveland, *Time Magazine*, April 5

Jimi Hendrix on stage at the Fillmore East, New York. *Elliott Landy.*

The Russian poet Yevgeny Yevtushenko, one of
the first Soviet dissenters, in Mexico City. *Inge Morath.*
Facing page. The Factory group posed around their leader,
Andy Warhol. Paul Morrissey, with curly hair, is standing above
and in the center, Viva is just above Warhol,
Taylor Mead is on his right, Nico, standing, is second from the right
and Fred Hugues is to the right of Nico. *Philippe Halsman.*

**Marcel Duchamp and Man Ray
at Man Ray's home in Paris.**
Henri Cartier Bresson.

The characteristic feature of public life in France at present is boredom. The French are bored. They take no part, either at close range or from a distance, in the great dramas that are convulsing the world. The Vietnam War worries them but does not affect them deeply. When invited to collect a billion for Vietnam, 20 francs a head, 33 francs for each adult, one year later they are still way off target. Moreover, apart from a few politically committed individuals, of whatever political stripe, everyone sees the war from more or less the same point of view. The Middle East conflict stirred up a little flurry of excitement at the beginning of last summer; the heroic onslaught provoked a wave of sympathy and some strong reactions; after six days, the fit was over. Latin-American guerrilla wars and the rumblings in Cuba were fashionable for a time; now they are just a subject of study for left-wing sociologists and for debate by intellectuals [...]

Boulevard Diderot, Paris.
Henri Cartier-Bresson

The young are bored. Students are demonstrating, stirring, fighting in Spain, Italy, Belgium, Algeria, Japan, America, Egypt, Germany even Poland. They feel that they have battles to fight, protests to register, or at least a sense of the absurd to oppose absurdity. French students are worrying about whether the girls on the Nanterre and Antony campuses should have unrestricted access to the boys bedrooms or not - surely a rather narrow interpretation of human rights. Young workers are looking for work but cannot find it… Fortunately, television is there to focus attention on more serious problems: Jean-Claude Killy's bank balance, expressway traffic jams, the national lottery - these are the subjects that take precedence on all French television networks every Sunday night. General de Gaulle is bored too. He vowed not to open any more flower shows, and there he is again, beaming officially, at the Salon de l'Agriculture at the Foire de Lyon. What else is there to do?

Pierre Viansson-Ponté, « Quand la France s'ennuie… », *Le Monde*, March 15

On the terrace at the Brasserie Lipp, Saint-Germain-des-Prés, Paris.
Henri Cartier-Bresson.

"Let it all hang out"
Paris, May.
Henri Cartier-Bresson

45

Top left: **Nicholas Ray at a meeting held in support of Henri Langlois.** *Bruno Barbey.*
Top right: **The Cinema Defense Committee set up
to support Henri Langlois. In the center, Jacques Prévert.** *Raymond Depardon.*
Bottom left: **Robert Bresson and François Truffaut.** *Raymond Depardon.*
Bottom right: **Jean Rouch, Jean Renoir and Jean-Luc Godard.** *Bruno Barbey.*

Today's powers-that-be do not accept independent thought or independent creativity; nor do they welcome the debate provoked by such independent activity, although it is one of the most valuable features of our humanist tradition. For example, when the Cinémathèque [French Film Institute] refuses to organize a festival of Iraqi or Argentinian films, this is found to be unacceptable, on the grounds that such a festival might be politically advantageous to the government. If this is the Fifth Republic's notion of culture, then the Ministry of Culture should be abolished. [...] The strength of the reaction throughout the country, and the importance of this demonstration show quite clearly that we do not mean to lose our fight for cultural liberty.

Pierre Mendès France,
lecture given in support of the Cinémathèque française,
March 21, *Cahiers du Cinéma* (April-May 1968)

Henri Langlois, founder and director of the Cinémathèque française,
was dismissed in February. The French cinema took up arms
under the banner of "Children of the Cinémathèque." This was one
of the events leading up to the upheavals of May 1968. *Henri Cartier Bresson.*

Alain Geismar, leader of the university
faculty union (SNESUP), in the Latin Quarter, Paris,
on the night of May 10. *Marc Riboud.*

The truth about the disturbances that took place during the night of May 10-11. At 2:15 a.m. the police brutally attacked the demonstrators using not only tear gas grenades but also chlorine and ammonia grenades, incendiary grenades and stun grenades...
The violence of the repression was such that numerous injured people had to be taken away. It is difficult at present to assess the number. When they had cleared the street, the CRS [French riot police] searched every building for demonstrators who had taken shelter.

Flyer from the CGT, FEN, CFDT and UNEF unions, May 11

The night of May 10,
in the Latin Quarter, Paris.
Bruno Barbey.

Automobiles burning
on the night of May 10.
Bruno Barbey.

152

Scenes in Paris
on the night of May 10.
Bruno Barbey.

The night of May 10
in the Latin Quarter. P
Bruno Barbey

Police barricade the Boulevard
Saint-Michel, Paris.
Henri Cartier-Bresson

Bystanders after
the rioting, Paris.
Henri Cartier-Bresson

Boulevard Saint-Michel at Place de la Sorbonne, Paris. *Bruno Barbey.*

Daniel Cohn-Bendit
at a meeting in the principal
auditorium of the Sorbonne.
Bruno Barbey.

In the courtyard of the Sorbonne
(PSU: Unified Socialist Party).
Martine Franck.

Jean-Paul Sartre at the Sorbonne.
Bruno Barbey.

At the Sorbonne, a debate between
artists and students.
Martine Franck.

The struggle against the police state goes on
To end repression, workers and students must win their freedom on the streets. As long as the cops are armed, students and workers must organize in self-defense to win the fight against organized repression.

Down with the police state
Down with capitalism
Up with socialism
Workers and students fight on the streets
Join the demonstration on Monday May 13, 1968
Gare de l'Est at 1:30 p.m.
Flyer, March 22 Movement, Paris, May 12

Maurice Grimaud, chief of the Paris police.
Raymond Depardon.

Protest march from Denfert-Rochereau to Nation by students and workers, Paris, May 13.
Bruno Barbey.

Alain Krivine leading a demonstration.
Bruno Barbey.

Alain Geismar and Jacques Sauvageot.
Marc Riboud.

Barricade on the Rue des Saints-Pères,
outside the Faculty of Medicine.
Raymond Depardon.

Above:
**Demonstrator arrested by the CRS,
the Arts et Métiers district, Paris.**
Henri Cartier-Bresson.

**The CRS in action,
Carrefour Mabillon, Paris.**
Bruno Barbey.

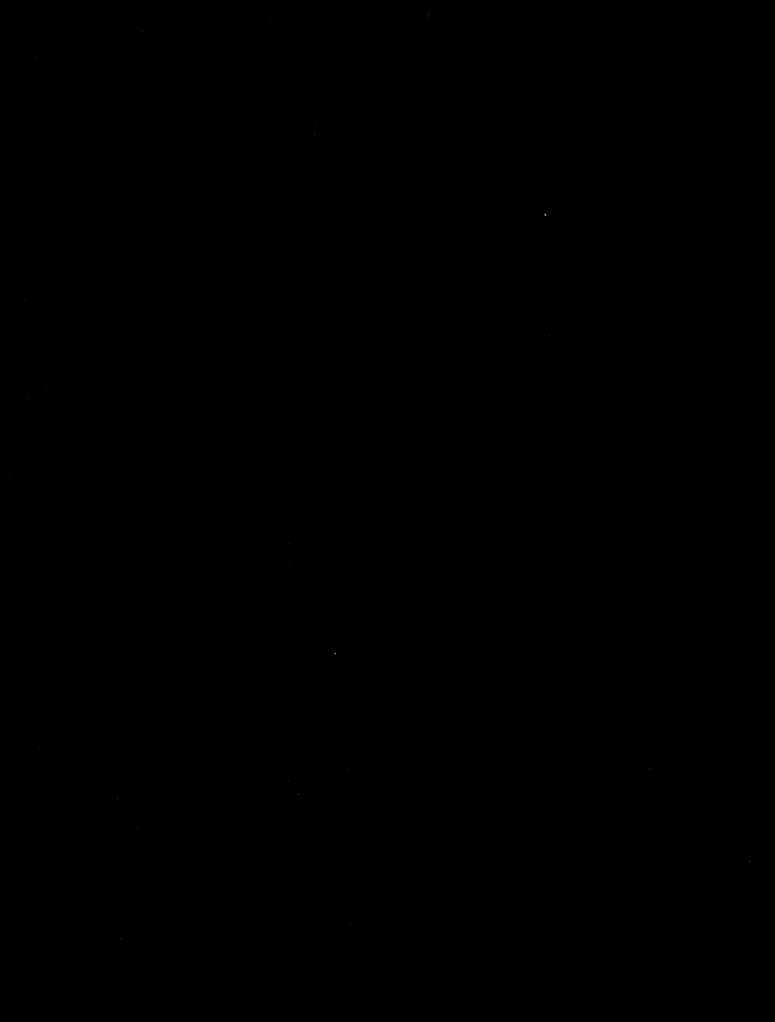

Ten years of Gaullism.
Centuries of exploitation.
Enough is enough.
What workers and
students want now is
power.
De Gaulle uses blandish-
ments and the big stick.
We know his big stick
well, by now. This is
incitement to civil war;
this is a move toward a
Fascist régime. De Gaulle
is not defending the
Republic or Democracy;
he is simply defending his
own régime, the régime
of the bourgeoisie. From
now on, he cannot stay in
power without organized
violence.
National French
Student's Union, May 30

Night protest
at the Renault factory,
Boulogne-Billancourt, May.
Bruno Barbey.

The CGT salutes the workers in their struggle, and in particular those of the publicly owned Renault works, who, in response to our appeal, have decided to strike and occupy the plant. The CGT calls on all workers to meet in the workplace with their union representatives to work out the conditions of their entry into the struggle and the claims on which their action will be based.

Appeal from the CGT labor union, May 16

Strikers at the Renault factory, Flins, May.
Martine Franck

"Workers, we must save ourselves."
To the ten million strikers, to all working people. Let no one speak for us. Let us continue our occupation of all workplaces.
To carry on the struggle, let us put all sectors of the economy affected by the strike at the service of the fighting workers. Let us now prepare the key points of our future power (direct supplies of necessities, plus organization of public services: transport, information, housing, etc.).
On the streets, in every committee, wherever we are, workers, peasants, laborers, students, teachers, high school students, let us organize and coordinate our struggle.
For the abolition of employers organizations
For worker power

Censier Collective, May 24

Striker at the Renault factory, Boulogne-Billancourt, May.
Martine Franck.

**Workers and students meet near the Renault factory,
Boulogne-Billancourt, May 17.** *Guy Le Querrec.*

17

Meeting at Charléty stadium organised by the PSU,
CFDT and FO, Unions, Paris, May 27. *Guy Le Querrec*

Men and women of France, as the custodian of national and republican legitimacy, I have, over the last twenty-four hours, considered all of the options, without exception, which would allow me to maintain that legitimacy. I have taken my decision. In the present circumstances, I shall not resign.

Address by General de Gaulle, May 30

Pierre Mendès France and Michel Rocard
during a demonstration,
avenue des Gobelins, Paris.
Martine Franck.

General de Gaulle during
his televised address, May 30.
Marc Riboud.

Graffiti at the Sorbonne, May:
"Comrades! Humanity will never find
happiness until the last capitalist has been
hanged with the guts of the last bureaucrat."
Guy Le Querrec.

CAMARADES!
l'humanité
ne sera heureuse
ue le jour où le
er capitaliste aura
endu avec les tripes
dernier bureauc

March in support of General de Gaulle,
from the Place de la Concorde
to the Arc de Triomphe,
Paris, May 30. *Martine Franck*

The extraordinary tidal wave of people moving inexorably up the processional way from Concorde to Etoile, is dotted with flags and with the symbol of the cross of Lorraine. The strains of the Marseillaise and the Chant du Départ can be heard at regular intervals. The rays of the setting spring sun light up a brilliantly colorful spectacle. The crowd fills the whole width of the Champs-Elysées, moving forward in a solid column more than fifty wide. As far as the eye can see, the great thoroughfare looks like a slow-moving ant heap, loudly proclaiming its confidence and trust in de Gaulle. All classes of society are there: the upper and lower middle classes. The store-keepers have been joined by a vast number of working-class people and even students. Although far from a majority, young people are not absent from this astonishing procession, preceded by cars decked out in blue, white and red.
A television news truck has disappeared from view beneath clusters of flag-waving marchers.

Le Figaro, May 31

As seen from the top of the Arc de Triomphe, the Gaullist demonstration fills the Champs-Elysées, May 30. *Bruno Barbey.*

Gaullist demonstration
on the Champs-Elysées, May 30.
Guy Le Querrec.

It's carnival time on the sidewalks of the Champs Elysées. All the Parisians who are milling around a chocolate vendor and in the elegant sidewalk cafés, which have stayed open, are making the V sign at each other, just as they did twenty-three years ago.

A group of very 16th Arrondissement [wealthy] old ladies — one of them in a wonderful candy-pink hat — are exchanging friendly gestures with a group of determined-looking militants who look like former "Red Berets" [like the American Green Berets]. A little further on a group of kids with piping voices are yelling slogans next to some tottering survivors of the 1914-18 War [...]

Gaullist demonstrators, May 30.
Guy Le Querrec.

186

The Rond-Point is filled with a seething mass of people who soon start moving forward again, chanting: Mitterrand, No Good; Communism Shall Not Pass, etc. Now and again someone can be heard shouting, Free the Sorbonne. Among the placards, one banner carried by a group of Gaullist students bears the words, Cohn-Bendit Go Home.

Le Figaro, May 31

Gaullist demonstrators, May 30.
Henri Cartier-Bresson.

We were attacked with night-sticks, to cries of "Into the water! All of you!" Comrades who were slow to take the plunge were pushed in with rifle stocks. On the other side of the Seine, cops were waiting for us with rifle stocks raised. Three times, comrades who showed signs of wanting to escape were told to "Stop or I shoot."
One comrade was pushed back into the river with the stock of a rifle. We saw Gilles going under. We shouted "Stop, someone's drowning!" The gendarmes looked on impassively.

Jean Terrel, former president of the UNEF student union, activist in the Union of Communist Youth (Marxist-Leninist), open letter to newspaper editors, *La Cause du Peuple*, nº. 15, June 12

The funeral of Gilles Tautin, a student who was drowned in the Seine near the Renault factory in Flins, after a police chase on June 10. Paris, June 15.
Bruno Barbey.

Massive support for Richard Nixon
at the Republican Convention,
Miami, August.
Elliott Erwitt.

Richard Milhous Nixon, the "old pro" of American politics, was nominated for President today on the first ballot at the Republican National Convention.

Mr. Nixon, only the eighth man to be renominated by the Republicans after having lost one Presidential election, triumphed over a determined "stop Nixon" drive waged from the left by Governor Rockefeller of New York and from the right by Governor Ronald Reagan of California. Just as the Nixon forces had steadfastly con-tended during a week of maneuvering at this 29th Republican National Convention, the 55-year-old former Vice-President, who was also the party's nominee in 1960, proved to have the 667 votes needed for nomination "buttoned up."

The New York Times, August 8

Republican Convention, Miami, August.
Elliott Erwitt.

Republican Convention
Miami, August.
Elliott Erwitt.

Demonstration against the Vietnam war during the Republican Convention.
In the center, Dr. Spock and his wife. The celebrated pediatrician maintained
that the war in Vietnam was unconstitutional, and that the methods of warfare used constituted a crime
against humanity. He was later indicted along with other intellectuals for incitement to resistance
to authority, found guilty, and then released. Washington, D.C., August. *Wayne Miller.*

This Monday, the Democratic Convention will open in Chicago in a very tense atmosphere. It faces the difficult task of nominating a candidate to stand against Richard Nixon in the November election. According to recent opinion polls, Hubert Humphrey still looks like the favorite. The peace candidates, Senators Eugene McCarthy and George McGovern, are way behind. Even farther behind is Lester Maddox, Governor of Georgia and mouthpiece of the supporters of segregation. Some of the delegates are still talking about a last-minute bid for reelection from Lyndon Johnson, though the President declared to a group of students in Texas on Saturday that he was not a candidate for anything, except perhaps a rocking chair.

Le Monde, August 27

The Democratic Convention in Chicago, August.
Raymond Depardon.

Mayor Daley and supporters raising their fists in defiance
at the anti-war demonstrators. Chicago, August.
Burt Glinn.
Supporters of the Democrats waving a banner with the words:
"Bobby [Robert Kennedy] we miss you."
Burt Glinn.

Some talk change.
Others cause it.

Humphrey

HUMPHREY

HUMPHREY

Support for Hubert Humphrey at
the Democratic Convention, Augus
Constantine Manos.

Anti-Vietnam war protests
during the Democratic Convention,
Chicago, August.
*From top: Raymond Depardon,
Roger Malloch,
Raymond Depardon.*

Just after 10 o'clock last night, National Guardsmen
fired a new barrage of light irritant gas into
demonstrators massed in Grand Park across
from the Conrad Hilton Hotel. [...]
And with the white gas still swirling in the air under the
bright television lights, the youths joined a guitarist in
an almost exultant chorus:
This land is your land, this land is my land.

J. Anthony Lukas, *The New York Times,* August 31

The American actor Dick Gregory, who gave up
his acting career to devote himself to politics,
demonstrating against the Vietnam war. *Burt Glinn.*

Michelangelo Antonioni during the
demonstrations in Chicago. *Bruce Davidson.*

During the Democratic Convention,
young anti-war protestors confront

Anti-Vietnam war protest, Grant Park:
supporters of the jailed Black Panther leader, Eldridge Cleaver.
Chicago, August. *Raymond Depardon.*

Anti-Vietnam war protest
Grant Park: in the center
William Burroughs
and Allen Ginsberg.
Chicago, August.
Roger Malloch.

To all the people of the Czechoslovak Socialist Republic

Yesterday, August 20, 1968, at about 11 PM, the armies of the Soviet Union, the Polish People's Republic, the German Democratic Republic, the Hungarian People's Republic and the Bulgarian People's Republic crossed the state borders of the Czechoslovak Socialist Republic. This took place without the knowledge of the President of the Republic [...]
or of the First Secretary of the Communist Party Central Comittee. The Presidium calls upon all citizens of the Republic to keep the peace and not resist the advancing armies, because the defense of our state borders is now impossible [...]
The presidium considers this action [the invasion] to be contrary to the fundamental principles of relations between socialist states and a denial of the basic norms of international law.

From *Prace* August 21

I happened to be on October Revolution Square, in the north of the city [Prague], at 4:30 a.m. when they appeared. They arrived in large numbers and at high speed, from the airfield where the Soviet Antonovs had deposited them some hours earlier. While they advanced towards the city, squads of parachute corpsmen in red berets dismounted from the tanks and took over the war ministry, which was right there on the square.

Philippa Hentges, *L'Humanité*, August 23

Wenceslas Square, in front of the National Museum, Prague.
Josef Koudelka.

A streetcar stop in Prague
with the announcement
of the 9 p.m. to 5 a.m. curfew
ordered under the state of siege.
Josef Koudelka.

Outside the radio station
Prague.
Josef Koudelka

Outside the
Prague.
Josef Koude

1

A demonstration is canceled to avoid handing the occupying forces a pretext for repression. Prague, August 22.
Josef Koudelka.

3

Today, as yesterday, the crowds in Wenceslas Square continued to taunt the invaders until nerves began to crack and morale to collapse. One Russian soldier was reduced to tears. The mass of people shouted ceaselessly at the invading troops: "your fathers came as liberators, you have come as oppressors," and "shame on you."

Reginald Peck, *Le Figaro*, August 26

I think this is the most peculiar occupation ever known in history, an occupation in which so many occupation soldiers have tears and sorrow and shame on their faces.

On Czechoslovak radio, August 24

Outside the radio station, Prague.
Josef Koudelka

Outside the radio station,
just before its occupation,
Prague.
Josef Koudelka.

Prague is still under occupation even though the occupiers withdrew from the center of the city today. People clench their fists as they walk past the National Museum and on Vinohradska Street. No, don't worry, we are not forgetting the year 1945 when Soviet troops liberated us. But we evaluate deeds justly. [...] They did not succeed in bringing the people of our country to their knees. We are the masters in our city. Go away!

Prazske Noviny, August

The Czechoslovak national flag.
Josef Koudelka

Fighting and barricades
outside the radio station,
Prague.
Josef Koudelka.

Vinohradska (formerly
Stalin) Avenue after
the fighting, Prague.

Protesting the Soviet invasion
at the St. Wenceslas monument,
Prague.
Josef Koudelka

BETCTCKИЙ ЦИРК OПЯТЬ В ПРА

Czechoslovak national flag decorated
with photographs of leaders
removed by the Russians.
Josef Koudelka.

Tension between Czechs
and occupying forces.
Ian Berry.

In the center of Prague.
Ian Berry.

22

Lenin, ever-present in posters and slogans:
"Wake up Lenin, Brezhnev has gone crazy!" *Josef Koudelka,*

As reported earlier, anti-socialist forces are trying to disturb normal life in the country and create complications by stirring up nationalistic passions and hostility toward the healthy, patriotic forces of the Czechoslovak people. [...]
The counterrevolutionary forces, particularly in Prague, are resorting to dangerous actions. Some statesmen in several bourgeois countries are beginning to take realistic positions. Illegal radio stations and publications are spreading falsifications of the lowest kind.

Report by Tass on the situation in Czechoslovakia from Pravda, August 23

Rude Pravo, official organ of the Communist Party.
Josef Koudelka.

The body of a young Czech, killed for having tried
to drape his flag over a Russian tank.
Josef Koudelka.

The Czechoslovaks must realize that their cause is our cause. We believe, with them, that Socialism must find an original form, although it may be a different form in each of our countries. We are fully aware — to return to the words of the call to arms of August 22 — that in proclaiming our solidarity with Czech writers, artists and intellectuals, we are defending Liberty, Progress and Socialism. Never have these attributes been mocked with such cynical effrontery as on August 21 of this year — a day of shame and anger.

Opus International, September

Vinohradska Avenue, Prague.
Josef Koudelka.

A thousand federal soldiers fired rifles and machine guns at what had been a peaceful student rally in the plaza of a housing project last night. When the shooting ended an hour later, the plaza and an adjacent Aztec ruin were strewn with bodies. [...] But it was virtually certain that at least 49 persons had been killed and 500 wounded. [...] The owner of a curio shop in the plaza said that soldiers had stolen much of her stock. There were five bullet holes in the windows of her store. Another woman said that drunken soldiers had rampaged through the project after the battle, looking for girls.

Paul L. Montgomery, *The New York Times*, October 4

Student demonstration in honor of the Cuban revolution, Mexico City, September.

"We both want you to print what I say the way I say it or not at all," said Carlos. "When we arrived there were boos. We want to make clear that white people seem to think black people are animals doing a job. We want people to understand that we are not animals or rats. We want you tell Americans and all the world that if they do not care what black people do they should not go to see black people perform.

"If you think we are bad, the 1972 Olympic Games are going to be mighty rough because Africans are winning all the medals."

International Herald Tribune, October 18

The 3,000 meter steeplechase
at the Olympic Games
in Mexico City, October.
Raymond Depardon.

Bob Beamon (at right in top photo),
who broke the Olympic long jump
record with a jump of 8.90 meters.
Raymond Depardon.

Tommie Smith and John Carlos.
Raymond Depardon.

Tommie Smith and John Carlos, gold and bronze medallists
at the Olympic Games in Mexico City; on the left,

stration escalated to arson at the National Railway Shinjuku Stati and the National Polic Agency decided to app "crimes of disturbanc rules. In the evening o the 21st, which was International Anti-War Day, more than 5000 Japanese Anti-Commu students behaved furiously at the Shinju Station, the Ministry o Defence and the Parliament. At the Shinjuku Station, thou sands of students and a throng of people occupied the railways peeling-off train seats barricading the platfor and setting fires, resulting in the burnin of platforms 3 & 4 and the roofs of the statio […] As of 0:15 on the 22nd

574 people had been arrested.

Mainichi Shimbun, October 22

Fall 1968 student
riots in Tokyo.
Bruno Barbey.

Fall 1968 student riots in Tokyo.
Hamaya Hiroshi (lower right) and Bruno Barbey

Tokyo street thronged
with student protesters,
fall 1968.
Bruno Barbey.

Nai Nam Bo and Xuan Thuy during peace talks,
Paris, May. *Fred Mayer.*

Hanoi, November 5. Five days
after the ceasefire in North Vietnam,
President Ho Chi Minh talks to Premier
Pham Van Dong, in the gardens
of the former palace of the governor
general of Indochina. On the same day,
Richard Nixon is elected President
of the United States.
Marc Riboud.

The funeral of the student Jan Palach,
who set fire to himself on Wenceslas Square
on January 16. Prague, January 25,1969. *Josef Koudelka.*

1968
MAGNUM
PHOTOGRAPHERS
ON ALL
FRONTS

Abbas
Eve Arnold
Bruno Barbey
Ian Berry
René Burri
Henri Cartier-Bresson
Bruce Davidson
Raymond Depardon
Elliott Erwitt
Martine Franck
Leonard Freed
Burt Glinn
Philip Jones-Griffiths
Thomas Hoepker
David Hurn
Josef Koudelka
Hiroji Kubota
Guy Le Querrec
Erich Lessing
Constantine Manos
Wayne Miller
Inge Morath
Marc Riboud
Ferdinando Scianna
Marilyn Silverstone
Dennis Stock
and Philippe Halsman
Hiroshi Hamaya
Elliott Landy
Herbert List
Don McCullin
Roger Malloch
Fred Mayer
distributed by Magnum

October 9 1967: Death of Che Guevara

October 21 1967: March on the Pentagon

CHRONOLOGY 1968

January

January 1: Exchanges of small-arms fire and shelling across the River Jordan between Israel and Jordan. U.S. Senator Edward F. Kennedy arrives in Saigon to study the problem of refugees and civilian war victims in Vietnam.

January 2: The National Liberation Front (NLF or Vietcong) attacks the U.S. base at Dan Tieng in Vietnam. Dr. Christian Barnard and his team perform their second heart transplant at the Grote Schuur Hospital in Cape Town. Bernard Bongo, President of the Republic of Gabon, makes his first official visit to France. In Paris, a Marxist-Leninist (i.e., Maoist) Communist Party is formed. In Havana, Fidel Castro announces that 1968 will be the Year of the Heroic Guerrilla Fighter, in memory of Che Guevara. In Guinea, President Sekou Touré is unanimously reelected for another seven-year term.

January 4: U.S. Secretary of State Dean Rusk declares that the administration takes Hanoi's preparedness to negotiate very seriously.

January 5: Antonin Novotny, President of the Republic of Czechoslavakia, is relieved of his post as first secretary of the Czechoslovak Communist Party at his own request, to be replaced by Alexander Dubcek, first secretary of the Communist Party of Slovakia; this marks the beginning of liberalization in Czechoslovakia. In Nigeria, military operations intensify against the breakaway state of Biafra.

January 7: Launch of the Surveyor 7 space probe at Cape Kennedy, Florida. Radio Sanaa announces that the Republic of Yemen requires foreign intervention to end the civil war.

January 8: Jean-Claude Killy wins the giant slalom at Adelboden, Switzerland.

January 11: In Washington, D. C., a United Black Front is formed on the initiative of Stokely Carmichael.

January 12: Violent clashes at Madrid University between police and students, who call an indefinite strike. Michel Deville is awarded the Prix Louis-Delluc for his film *Benjamin ou les Mémoires d'un puceau*.

January 14: There is a rumor that President Lyndon B. Johnson has written to President Ho Chi Minh to ask for details of any peace initiative.

January 15: There are clashes at universities in France, notably Caen and Nanterre.

January 17: U.S. military strength in Thailand increases to 43,000 men, 33,000 of whom belong to the Air Force.

January 18: In Geneva, the USSR and the United States present a treaty on the nonproliferation of nuclear weapons. In Mozambique, for the first time, a bishop preaches in a mosque.

January 19: In France, Robert Poujade is elected leader of the UDR (Union for the Defence of the Republic). In Hot Creek Valley, Nevada, U.S. scientists and engineers carry out the largest underground nuclear test ever, in a shaft 975 meters deep.

January 20: The U.S. Army is now 3.5 million strong. South Vietnam is dropped from the list of 123 countries receiving technical assistance under the UN development program.

January 21: Vietcong offensive in the north-west of South Vietnam. Jean-Claude Killy wins the combined skiing-event at Kitzbühel (Austria).

January 22: A North Korean commando force succeeds in entering Seoul.

January 23: The patrol boat U.S.S. Pueblo is seized by North Korea in the Sea of Japan.

January 24: The U.S. Seventh Fleet on red alert in the Sea of Japan.

January 25: The U.S. base at Khe Sanh, near Saigon, is besieged by North Vietnamese forces. In New York, the guru Maharishi Mahesh Yogi is fêted by his Hippie followers.

January 26: Violent demonstrations by strikers at the Saviem works in Caen. On the same day, incidents at Fougères and at the University of Nanterre. Arthur Penn's film *Bonnie and Clyde* scores a hit in Paris.

January 27: In Athens, the composer Mikis Theodorakis is released from prison. As a left-wing activist, he had been arrested after the Colonels Coup of April 21, 1967.

January 29: In Washington, President Johnson presents a record budget of $186.1 billion for the financial year 1968-69; defense's share is $79.8 billion, including $26.3 billion for the Vietnam War. Secret talks between the U.S. and Soviets at the United Nations in New York on the Pueblo question.

January 30: Bilateral agreement between Czechoslovakia and the USSR on a package of economic and social reforms in Czechoslovakia. In Prague, there is a proposal to allow the importation of newspapers from Western Europe.

January 31: In Saigon, a Vietcong offensive reaches the gates of the U.S. Embassy; a state of siege is proclaimed. Widespread attacks in the Mekong Delta. France returns the base of Mers el-Kebir to Algeria, nine years ahead of the date specified in the Evian independence agreement of 1962.

February

February 1: Opening of the second United Nations Conference on Trade and Development (UNCTAD) in New Delhi; 132 countries are represented. In Hue, the former imperial capital of Annam, the Vietcong establish a revolutionary government; Vietcong soldiers are seen publicly for the first time in certain areas of Saigon.

February 2: In Algiers, 8,000 students go on strike to protest government influence on their union. The university closes on 4 February.

February 3: After four days of fierce fighting, pockets of Vietcong remain in Saigon. In France, André Malraux inaugurates the ultramodern Maison de la Culture, Grenoble.

February 4: The Vietcong still hold the citadel of Hue. In Kinshasa, President Mobutu of the Congo proposes a United States of Central Africa, to include the Congo, Chad and the Central African Republic.

February 5: In Berlin, the 500th soldier of the People's Army of the German Democratic Republic escapes to the West.

February 6: Opening of the tenth Winter Olympics in Grenoble. U.S. Marines recapture Hue, except for the citadel. In Algiers, police clear the university campus, occupied by hundreds of striking students.

February 7: A crisis, provoked by the insistence of Flemish Christian-Socialist deputies that French-speaking students be excluded from the Catholic University of Louvain, triggers the resignation of the Belgian prime minister. First official visit to France by General Aref, President of the Republic of Iraq. In France, the Vietnam committees organize a demonstration against a meeting held in support of US intervention in Vietnam. Violent clashes with the police. Demonstration in Paris in support of the Vietcong. Using Soviet tanks, the North Vietnamese seize a position between Saigon and Khe Sanh.

February 8: In the Middle East, more attacks on the Israeli-occupied territories. The U.S. President asks Congress for $100 million more to provide military aid for South Korea. Hanoi declares itself willing to commence negotiations once U.S. bombing has ceased.

February 9: Fighting continues in Saigon. President Nguyen Van Thieu of South Vietnam requests dictatorial powers for a year. Student demonstrations in Warsaw.

February 10: The Beatles leave for India to study and practice meditation.

February 11: In Bordeaux, joint demonstration by Dassault factory workers and university students. More than half a million refugees enter South Vietnam in a few days.

February 12: President Johnson announces that he is willing to meet the North Vietnamese for talks as soon as possible.

February 13: U.S. forces bomb Vietcong positions in the suburbs of Saigon, in spite of an eighteen-day ceasefire declared by the U.S. over North Vietnam. Marielle Goitschel wins gold medal for slalom in the winter Olympics in Grenoble.

February 14: Incidents in various universities. General de Gaulle holds talks with U Thant, secretary general of the United Nations, on the Vietnam situation.

February 15: Unrest at the University of Madrid.

February 17: In Addis Ababa, African countries announce their intention of boycotting the Olympic Games if South Africa is allowed to participate.

February 18: In West Berlin, 10,000 students, led by Rudi Dutschke, demonstrate against the Vietnam War. At the Winter Olympics in Grenoble, now drawing to a close, Jean-Claude Killy achieves his objective and wins the alpine ski triathlon (downhill February 9; giant slalom, February 12; special slalom February 18).

February 19: The border dispute between India and Pakistan over the Rann of Kutch is settled at the International Court of Justice in The Hague.

February 21: The Belgian Parliament is dissolved. Elections are set for March 31. The anti-Vietnam war rally in West Berlin is countered by a large demonstration for Peace and Liberty.

February 23: Vietcong resistance in Hue collapses after more than three weeks fighting against U.S. and allied forces. In Paris, agitation over access to student dormitories: male and female students claim the right to free access to all buildings.

February 24: In France, the FGDS (Federation of the Democratic and Socialist Left) and Communists adopt a joint plan of action. The first U.S. bombing mission takes place over the port of Hanoi. In New York, H. Rap Brown, leader of the Black Power movement, advocates a black revolution so black people can live. In Cairo, students demonstrate in favor of press freedom. The university closes for three weeks.

February 25: Famine in Hue following the destruction of the city and surrounding areas.

February 26: In France, high-school teachers go on strike, and the first meeting of the Comités d'Action lycéens (CAL, High School Student Action Committees) is held. Israel accepts the principle of a UN-brokered settlement of the Middle East conflict. In Tokyo, demonstrators protest the construction at Narita of an airfield for use by U.S. aircraft carrying nuclear weapons.

February 27: In Bahrein, the plan for a federation of the Persian Gulf States, proposed by Abu Dhabi and Dubai, is approved by seven other Emirates.

March

March 1: In Saigon, the parliament refuses to grant dictatorial powers to the government. In Washington, the Consultative Commission set up by President Johnson after the race riots in Denver recommends that segregation in housing be made illegal, that artificial barriers to employment be dismantled and that two million new jobs be created. In Czechoslovakia, censorship is abolished. In Rome, 200 people are injured in clashes between students and the police.

March 9: In Poland, violent clashes between students and police during freedom demonstrations.

March 10: Mauritius gains its independence, becoming the 124th member of the United Nations. The United States asks allies (Australia, New Zealand, Thailand and Korea) to assist with military reinforcements for Vietnam. U.S. Senator Eugene J. McCarthy, who favors an unconditional end to U.S. bombing in Vietnam, wins 42 percent of Democratic votes in the New Hampshire primary.

March 13: In Czechoslovakia the regime begins to liberalize: censorship slackens and former police chief Mamula is arrested. A U.S. State Department spokesperson announces that the administration has embarked on a wide-ranging review of its Vietnam policy.

March 15: The National Council of Slovakia demands a new constitution to set up a Socialist federation.

March 16: In the United States, Senator Robert F. Kennedy becomes a candidate for the Democratic presidential nomination. "Dock of the Bay" by Otis Redding (died December 10, 1967) leads world record sales.

March 18: In Poland, steelworkers in Nowa Huta come out on strike in sympathy with the striking students in Cracow. Police arrest 1,208 people, including 367 students. On March 24 the Polish bishops intervene as mediators between protestors and the authorities, in the hope of hastening the fundamental reforms demanded by the people. The unrest persists, however, and on March 30 the authorities close the University of Warsaw. The U.S. Defense Department reveals that since 1963 more than 100,000 tons of napalm have been discharged over Vietnam.

March 20: The Vatican and the World Council of Churches join forces to demand the cessation of hostilities in Nigeria. Denmark, Finland, Norway and Sweden form a peacekeeping force to be put at the disposal of the UN.

March 21: In reprisals against al-Fatah (a palestinian liberation organization), the Israeli army bombs a Palestinian refugee camp in Jordan: 200 people are killed. Willy Brandt is reelected leader of the Social Democrat Party in West Germany. Christian de Chalonges is awarded the Prix Jean-Vigo for his film *O Salto*.

March 22: The Mansholt Plan, drawn up to deal with overproduction of milk in the European Economic Community (EEC), is withdrawn after adverse reactions from farmers. Incidents at the university of Nanterre: after the arrest of students who took part in demonstrations against the American war in Vietnam, their fellow-students occupy the administrative buildings, creating the March 22 Movement led by Daniel Cohn-Bendit. Antonin Novotny, President of Czechoslovakia since 1967, resigns and is replaced by General Svoboda.

March 23: Dubcek, the Czechoslovak Communist Party leader, liberalizes the press and all literary and academic production. The French rugby team celebrates its first grand slam in the Five Nations tournament in Cardiff.

March 24: The U.S. base at Khe Sanh comes under heavy fire; U.S. bombers counterattack.

March 25: Widespread student strikes in Italy.

March 27: The Russian cosmonaut Yuri Gagarin, the first man in space (in 1961), is killed in a plane crash. At Nanterre, classes in the faculty of letters are suspended for several days after serious disturbances. The Indonesian parliament unanimously elects General Suharto as President of the Republic for a five-year term.

March 28: In Brussels, the EEC fails to bring the Common Market in milk and beef into operation in time for April 1; it is postponed until June 1. In Memphis, a civil rights march led by the Rev. Dr. Martin Luther King, Jr. ends with a riot. The faculty of letters at Nanterre university is closed. In Japan, demonstration against a hospital intended to receive U.S. war wounded from Vietnam.

March 29: General Svoboda elected by the national assembly to be President of the Czechoslovak Republic. In Warsaw, the rector of the university closes seven faculties.

March 30: In Detroit a congress of black nationalists publishes a declaration of independence and a plan for a separate black Republic of Songhay, made up of Mississippi, Alabama, Georgia, South Carolina and Louisiana.

March 31: President Johnson announces an end to bombing missions over most of North Vietnam, plus his own withdrawal from the electoral campaign. In Japan, 4,800 police are deployed against 1,400 left-wing students protesting the construction of an airfield to supply the U.S. forces in Vietnam. General Gowon, head of the Nigerian government, states that the backbone of the Biafran rebellion has been broken. In legislative elections in Belgium, the followers of Van den Boeynants gain ground in all three major parties.

April

April 1: The occupation of Rome University ends.

April 2: Further disturbances at the University of Nanterre, which contin throughout the month. In Kinshas Presidents Mobutu, Bokassa an Tombalbaye sign the charter of th United States of Central Africa. Senat McCarthy wins another primary, th time in Wisconsin.

April 3: General de Gaulle describ President Johnson's decision to call halt to bombing raids in North Vietna as a first step along the road to peac Hanoi agrees to open negotiations wi the U.S.

April 4: The Rev. Martin Luther Kin leader of the black civil rights mov ment, is assassinated by James Ea Ray on the balcony of his hotel Memphis, Tennessee. The Rev. Ralph Abernathy takes his place on the san day. On April 11, President Johns signs the 1968 civil rights legislatio which prohibits discrimination again the black population. Civil unrest aft the murder of Rev. King leaves 4 people dead and several hundrec injured in a number of U.S. cities. pitched battle between students ar police in Rio de Janeiro. The centr committee of the Czechoslovak Con munist Party appoints Oldrich Cerni an economist, to form a new go ernment.

April 5: The Czechoslovak Communi Party decides to rehabilitate the victim of the purges and show trials of 195 54 and to revoke the expulsions writers carried out in 1967.

April 6: In Warsaw, the government co tinues its purge of Zionists, revisio ists and other enemies of the State.

April 7: U.S. and South Vietnames troops lift the two-month siege of th Khe Sanh base. Jim Clark, the Englis racing driver, is killed in a race at Hoc enheim, West Germany. Eddy Merc wins the Paris-Roubaix bicycle race.

April 8: Repression of the prote movement in Poland.

April 9: In Atlanta, more than 150,0 people, including Vice President Hub H. Humphrey, attend the funeral Martin Luther King. First rocket laun at Kourou, French Guiana of the Fren space program.

April 10: President Nguyen Van Thieu of South Vietnam orders mobilization of all South Vietnamese between the ages of 18 and 45. General Abrams succeeds General Westmoreland as U.S. commander in Saigon.

April 11: On a West Berlin street, the German student leader Rudi Dutschke is shot three times in the head and seriously wounded.

April 12: In Poland, purges take place in the administration, the press, and the scientific and cultural establishment.

April 13: Violent student demonstrations in Berlin in response to the attempt on Rudi Dutschke's life. Tanzania declares its recognition of Biafra.

April 14: Former U.S. Secretary of Defense, Robert S. McNamara, offers his support to Robert F. Kennedy's presidential campaign. Russian scientists successfully dock two unmanned satellites, Cosmos 212 and Cosmos 213, launched 12 hours apart. Still docked, the two satellites make a soft landing in Kazakhstan two days later.

April 15: Revelations about past oppression by the Communist regime in Czechoslovakia begin to emerge. In Damascus the name of the al-Fatah leader is revealed: Yasser Arafat, an engineer with a degree from the University of Cairo.

April 20: Pravda castigates the ideological deviations rife in some European Communist Parties.

April 21: Scuffles between leftist and rightist students at the general assembly of the French National Students Union (UNEF).

April 22: Pierre Elliott Trudeau becomes Prime Minister of Canada. Senator Eugene McCarthy denounces the dangerous expansion of military influence in American politics.

April 24: In Algiers, President Boumédienne comes under automatic fire as he leaves a cabinet meeting, and narrowly escapes with his life.

April 25: The 1968 acting Oscars are awarded to two American stars, Rod Steiger and Katharine Hepburn.

27 April: Vice President Humphrey declares his candidacy for the Democratic presidential nomination. South Africa is banned from the Olympic Games in Mexico by the International Olympic Committee (IOC). In Paris, Daniel Cohn-Bendit is arrested.

28 April: The U.S. turns down Phnom Penh and Warsaw as venues for the Vietnam peace talks.

30 April: Governor Nelson A. Rockefeller of New York State announces his candidacy for the Republican presidential nomination, in opposition to Richard M. Nixon.

May

May 1: The French Communist Party and its affiliated labor union (the CGT) stage marches, which pass without disturbance. Speaking to a mixed audience of students, Mr. McKissick, national director of the Congress for Racial Equality (C.O.R.E.), pledges his support for Stokely Carmichael and H. Rap Brown, the Black Power advocates.

May 2: On the Nanterre campus, an Anti-Imperialist Day is organized. The dean suspends classes. French Prime Minister, Georges Pompidou, visits Iran and Afghanistan. In Memphis, the Poor People's March on Washington, interrupted by the murder of Martin Luther King, resumes.

May 3: In Paris, at the request of Jean Roche, rector of the university, police evacuate the Sorbonne using tear gas. Violent clashes in the Latin Quarter: 100 injured, 596 arrested.

May 4: The leaders of Czechoslovakia, Dubcek and Cernik, visit Moscow. Classes suspended at the Sorbonne in Paris and student bodies call an indefinite strike for the liberation of all their arrested comrades.

May 5: Thirteen people arrested during a demonstration in Paris are convicted and four of them jailed. Vietcong offensive south of the 17th Parallel.

May 6 Closure of all university premises in Paris brings 49,000 students out into the streets; police strength is 20,000. Street barricades are set up in the Latin Quarter, and violent clashes leave 945 injured (including 345 police); 422 arrests are made. In London, the Nigerians and Biafrans enter their first round of peace talks under the supervision of the Secretary General of the Commonwealth.

May 7: Paris: 30,000 students join in a long march. The Internationale is sung around the Tomb of the Unknown Soldier; most French universities lend their support.

May 8: The situation in the universities is debated in the French National Assembly, and 25,000 students stage a peaceful march. Robert F. Kennedy wins the Indiana primary. The Nigerians and Biafrans choose Kampala, Uganda, for substantive talks, to begin on May 23. Gabon officially recognizes Biafra. Julien Clerc's first single, "La Cavalerie," reaches the French charts.

May 9: Disturbances in Strasbourg, Nantes, Rennes and Toulouse. In Lyon and Dijon, workers join the students. In Paris, Alain Peyrefitte, the Minister of Education, forbids the rector to reopen the faculties. Warsaw Pact forces begin maneuvers on the Czechoslovak border.

May 10: Sixty barricades erected in Paris, some of them 3 meters (10 feet) high. At 2:15 a.m., the CRS (French riot police) attack the barricade on Rue Gay-Lussac with tear gas grenades; in the morning there are 720 people with slight injuries, 367 seriously injured, including 251 policemen, 468 detained, and 80 burnt-out vehicles.

May. 11: The French labor unions call a general strike for May 14. In West Germany, student organizations and labor unions demonstrate against the government's emergency powers bill.

May 12: Georges Pompidou returns from Afghanistan, orders the Sorbonne reopened on the following day and announces that the convicted students will be heard in the Court of Appeals. In Strasbourg, the red flag flies over the student occupied faculty of letters. Professor Charles Dubost performs a successful heart transplant on a priest, Father Boulogne.

May 13: In Paris, 800,000 demonstrators (according to the labor unions) or 171,000 (according to the police) march from Place de la République to Place Denfert-Rochereau. Marches outside Paris are joined by Socialist politicians, including Pierre Mendès France, François Mitterrand, Guy Mollet and Waldeck-Rochet. The general strike wins massive support. The red flag flies over the Sorbonne. First plenary talks between the U.S. and North Vietnam.

May 14: The Sorbonne declares its independence and the faculty of Nanterre its autonomy. Near Nantes, nearly 2,000 workers at Sud-Aviation detain the chief executive of their company. General de Gaulle leaves for an official trip to Romania.

May 15: Warsaw Pact military maneuvers in Czechoslovakia announced for June. Students occupy the university of Milan. In Munich, violent demonstrations leave two people dead. In Paris, 2,500 students occupy the Odéon theater, whose director, Jean-Louis Barrault, supports their cause. The Ivory Coast officially recognizes Biafra.

May 16: Renault factory workers strike and fly the red flag. Unrest spreads to the Paris transit authority and the French national railroads. France is gradually paralyzed. The first European satellite, Esro II, designed for the study of solar and cosmic radiation, is launched at Vandenberg air base in the U.S.

May 17: In France, Georges Séguy, Secretary General of the CGT, demands higher wages and a cut in working hours; he rejects the students offer to amalgamate.

May 18: Two million workers now on strike in France. De Gaulle returns from Bucharest twenty-four hours early. Nigerian troops capture Port Harcourt, capital of Biafra. In South Vietnam, Prime Minister Nguyen Van Loc resigns and is replaced by Tran Van Houong.

May 19: At his official residence, the Elysée palace, General de Gaulle declares reform, yes, chaos, no! The Cannes Film Festival is canceled because of political unrest.

May 20: The Paris transit unions demand unbiased reporting on television. Unrest in the textile and chemical industries and in the dockyards. Four to six million French workers now estimated to be out on strike. According to public opinion polls, 53 percent of the inhabitants of Paris consider the student protests justified. Zambia officially recognizes Biafran independence.

May 21: The UN Security Council calls on Israel to withdraw from the Jordanian sector of Jerusalem; the U.S. and Canada abstain. The French franc collapses; capital begins to flow from France to Switzerland. Housewives start stockpiling food and drivers stampede for gas. Eight to ten million workers now on strike. The French employers organization headquarters is occupied for two hours by a force of junior executives. General de Gaulle has separate meetings with Averell Harriman, leader of the U.S. delegation to the Vietnam talks, and Xuan Thuy, leader of the North Vietnamese delegation.

May 22: French government grants amnesty for actions committed by students during demonstrations. The National Assembly throws out a left-wing opposition censure motion against the government. Labor unions declare willingness to negotiate with employers and government. Daniel Cohn-Bendit is declared a prohibited immigrant in France and leaves for Germany. Demonstrating in Paris, his supporters chant: "We are all German Jews."

May 23: Writers occupy the Société des Gens de Lettres in Paris. Student demonstrations in Italy, Belgium and Holland.

May 24: Riots in Lyon; a police officer, Inspector Lacroix, is killed by a truck set in motion by students. In Paris, the CGT union holds a peaceful march. At 8 p.m., President de Gaulle announces that a referendum on worker participation will be conducted in June. After his speech, violent clashes take place at a principal train station, the Gare de Lyon, in Paris; there is arson at the Stock Exchange;

three police stations are attacked; 4⁵ are injured, and 795 arrests are mad Committees for the Defense of th Republic are formed to try to bring t chaos under control.

May 25: Georges Pompidou brin employers and unions together on r de Grenelle. Discussions continue un May 27. The state broadcasting ne work, ORTF, joins the strikers.

May 27: The rue de Grenelle agreemen on a minimum wage, reductions working hours, a lower retirement a and the principle of union represent tion in management are rejected by t union rank and file. At 5 p.m., 30,0 students and young workers march fr the Gobelins tapestry works to t Charléty sport stadium, where they h a meeting at which Pierre Mend France is present; the leftist PS (Unified Socialist Party) and numero members of the CFDT union al participate.

May 28: François Mitterrand announc that he will stand as candidate f President of the Republic should vacancy occur; he proposes the creati of a provisional government und Pierre Mendès France. The Communis have their reservations. The resignati of Alain Peyrefitte, French Minister Education, handed in on 11 May, tak effect. In spite of the prohibiti against his return, Cohn-Bendit rea pears in France and holds a press co ference at the Sorbonne. In Nante violent confrontations with the polic The Biafrans reject Nigerian proposal and the Nigerian government refuses allow food supplies to reach the Biafr refugees.

May 29: Bloodshed at the University Dakar, Senegal. In Belgium, stude protests disrupt radio and televisi programs. In Frankfurt, students occu the university, rededicating it to K Marx. A demonstration by the CGT uni in Paris attracts several hundr thousand participants. Pierre Mend France declares himself ready to form provisional government if given t support of the united left. Anton Novotny is expelled from the Centr

Committee of the Communist Party in Czechoslovakia.

May 30: De Gaulle declares the national assembly dissolved and announces that elections will be held in June. The referendum planned for June 16 is postponed. One million Parisians demonstrate their support of General de Gaulle in a rally from the Concorde to the Etoile.

May 31: Georges Pompidou sets up a transitional government; legislative elections are set for June 23 and 30. Gasoline begins to become available again. Gaullist demonstrations throughout France. A state of emergency is declared in Senegal. Negotiations between Nigerians and Biafrans, begun in Kampala in early May, collapse. The universities of Rome and Milan are occupied.

June

June 1: After the success of "The Sound of Silence," the singing partnership of Paul Simon and Art Garfunkel scores an international hit with "Mrs. Robinson."

June 2: Violent student demonstrations in Belgrade. Heavy Vietcong mortar bombardment of Saigon.

June 4: Violent clashes in the faculty of letters in Lyon.

June 6: In France, work begins again in the public sector and in many private businesses. In Los Angeles, Robert F. Kennedy, shot by Sirhan Sirhan as he celebrates his victory in the California and South Dakota primaries, dies of his injuries. The assassin, a Palestinian immigrant to America, gives Kennedy's sympathy with Israel as the reason for his attack.

June 7: Near San Sebastian, José Pardines Azcay, a policeman, is the first victim of the Basque separatist movement, ETA. The Académie Française awards its annual literary prize to Henri Bosco.

June 9: After student demonstrations in Belgrade, Marshal Joseph Broz Tito pledges political and social reform.

June 10: At Flins, near Paris, during violent clashes at the Renault factory

(which began on 7 June), a high school student, Gilles Tautin, drowns in the Seine. There are still a million workers on strike in France, and now university staff join them.

June 11: In Paris, demonstrations at the Gare de l'Est and in the Latin Quarter after the Flins incident: 400 injured, 1,500 arrested, 72 barricades. A demonstrator is killed by a bullet outside the Peugeot factory in Montbéliard. High school classes resume.

June 12: The French government decides to impose a ban on demonstrations throughout the country and to disband eleven revolutionary groups. In Biafra, the blockade imposed by the Nigerian troops drives more than a million people to the brink of starvation. In Belgium, after 27 days of crisis, Gaston Eyskens forms a new government. Eddy Merckx is the first Belgian to win the Giro (Italian bicycle race).

June 14: Police evacuate the Odéon theater.

June 15: Troubles in the universities of Zurich, Bern, Brussels, Belgrade, Istanbul, Dakar and Kinshasa, as well as in Latin America.

June 16: The Sorbonne is evacuated.

June 18: More than 100,000 metal workers start to return to work in France, most importantly at Renault. Disturbances in Latin America universities, in Uruguay, Argentina, Chile, Ecuador, Colombia and Mexico. In Nigeria, 300,000 civilians have been killed in less than a year.

June 20: Warsaw Pact maneuvers begin in Czechoslovakia.

June 23: In France, the first round of elections to the legislature show an appreciable drop in votes for the Communists and the left-wing federation, and a definite swing to the center: 142 of the 154 seats settled in the first round go to the ruling coalition.

June 24: The police clear Resurrection City, the camp founded in Washington, D.C. by participants in the Poor People's March that began on May 2. Ralph Abernathy, leader of the protest, is arrested.

June 25: The process of democratization

in Czechoslovakia, the Prague Spring, continues. The Czech national assembly votes in favor of rehabilitating the victims of political trials since 1948, the date when the Communists seized power, also voting them financial compensation. The 2,000-Word Manifesto, published on June 27, arouses enormous interest at home and abroad. Seventy artists, scientists and athletes, including Emil Zatopek, Jiri Raska and Vera Caslavska, have signed a declaration in favor of democratization. Dubcek's government comes out in favor of the manifesto. Student demonstrations in São Paulo, Brazil.

June 26: After the resignation of Prime Minister Aldo Moro in Italy, Giovanni Leone, of the Christian Democratic Party, forms a new government. U.S. troops evacuate the Khe Sanh base.

June 27: In Moscow, the journal of the Writers Union publishes a virulent attack on Alexander Solzhenitsyn, whose novel, *Cancer Ward*, is a huge success abroad.

June 30: The second round of the legislative elections in France confirms the success of the ruling coalition, which gains 358 of the 485 seats in the new national assembly. Within the ruling group, the Gaullists take 97 seats and the Independent Republicans 21. The Left-Wing Federation loses 61 seats, the Communist Party 39, the Center Party 8 and the leftist PSU all three of its elected members, including Pierre Mendès France, who is defeated in Grenoble.

July

July 1: The customs services of the six member countries of the EEC are unified eighteen months earlier than the date specified in the Treaty of Rome.

July 3: In Bucharest, the Communist leader, Nicolae Ceausescu, calls for the abolition of all military blocs.

July 5: In Prague, publication of the 1,000-Word Manifesto (following the earlier 2,000-Word Manifesto), refuting the claim that the democratization process is at an end. In preparation for quitting Japanese bases on Okinawa, the U.S. builds new air bases in South Korea. In Paris, the faculty of medicine is cleared by police.

July 10: Maurice Couve de Murville, foreign minister since 1958, replaces Georges Pompidou as Prime Minister. His new ministry is formed on July 13. U Thant declares that the UN is unable to intervene in the Nigeria-Biafra conflict because it is an internal matter.

July 12: Moscow announces the end of military exercises carried out with its allies on Polish, Czechoslovakian and Soviet soil. Former General Salan, imprisoned for life for his part in the attempted coup in Algiers in 1962, former Colonel Argoud, and ten other detainees are granted an amnesty by General de Gaulle, to coincide with Bastille day.

July 13: Ralph Abernathy, director of the Southern Christian Leadership Conference (SCLC) and organizer of the Poor People's March, is freed from jail.

July 15: In Warsaw, the Communist leaders Brezhnev, Kosygin, Podgorny (all USSR), Zhivkov (Bulgaria), Ulbricht (GDR), Kadar (Hungary), and Gomulka and Cyrankiewicz (Poland) meet to discuss developments in Czechoslovakia. The outcome is a severe warning delivered to Prague, where it is received as an ultimatum. Direct flights from New York to Moscow are inaugurated. In the House of Lords, in London, the Archbishop of Canterbury demands an immediate halt to arms shipments to Nigeria.

July 17: Maurice Couve de Murville presents his government and program in the French National Assembly; he promises major reforms, to begin before Christmas, and a stable economy within eighteen months. In Iraq, General Hassan al-Bakr stages a coup, overthrowing General Aref.

July 18: Alexander Dubcek reasserts his intention to continue with reforms in Czechoslovakia. A few days later, however, he is obliged to accept an invitation from the Soviet Communist Party to attend friendly bilateral talks, to take place in Cierna, Slovakia. A Biafran

delegation arrives in Niger hoping, with the assistance of the Consultative Council of the Organization of African Unity, to find a peace formula to end the civil war in Nigeria.

July 19: Waldeck-Rochet, secretary general of the French Communist Party, visits Moscow and Prague; Luigi Longo, his Italian counterpart, visited the same two capitals on July 16.

July 22: An article by the physician Andrei Sakharov denouncing the politics of the USSR is published in the New York Times.

July 23: Race riots in Cleveland, Ohio: eight killed.

July 25: Stanley Kubrick's film *2001: a Space Odyssey* has its first screening.

July 26: Failure of discussions on the creation of a peace corridor between Biafrans and Nigerians. Racial disturbances in New York, Seattle, Chicago, Cleveland.

July 27: In Mexico, a demonstration by students protesting against bestial and sadistic repression by the granaderos (paramilitary police) three days earlier: 8 killed, 500 injured.

July 28: Bertrand Russell (Lord Russell) attacks the British Government for continuing to supply arms to Nigeria.

July 29: Opening of the talks between the Soviet Union and Czechoslovakia in Cierna. Pope Paul VI's condemnation of contraception and abortion provokes a lively response.

July 30: In Mexico, further violent clashes between police and students; the police take over the university premises. EEC foreign ministers postpone consideration of Great Britain's application for membership until the autumn.

July 31: In France, reorganization of ORTF (French national television service); large numbers of journalists lose their posts.

August

August 1: In Mexico, a demonstration by 100,000 students takes place without disturbance.

August 3: Military coup in Brazzaville, in

the (formerly French) Republic Congo. Almost half the members of the national assembly in South Vietna vote for direct negotiations between the two Vietnams.

August 4: Israeli air raid on Pales tinian commando camps in Jorda Jordan appeals to UN Security Council.

August 5: Negotiations between Niger and Biafra begin in Addis Ababa.

August 8: In the United States, Richard Nixon is nominated as presidential candidate at the Republican Par convention. In Los Angeles, exchange gunfire between police and Blac Panthers. In Mexico, students vote for general strike and the cancellation end-of-year examinations to protest the government's intransigent attitude.

August 9: Official visit to Prague Marshal Tito.

August 10: The Nigerian milita command forces the International Re Cross to cease its mercy flights Biafra, where fighting is principal harming the civilian population. Ac cording to the Red Cross, 8 to 10,00 people are dying of hunger in Biafra refugee camps every day. Marshal Tit assures the Czechoslovak governmen of his support.

August 11: A communiqué from Mosco announces that military maneuvers the Soviet, Polish and East Germa armies will take place in the GDF Poland and the Ukraine. After a month pause, the U.S. resumes bombing raid on North Vietnam.

August 12: The East German head state, Walter Ulbricht, visits Czecho slovakia. In Addis Ababa, the Nigeria delegation rejects Biafran proposals fo the recognition of Biafra as a independent state.

August 15: Nicolae Ceausescu visit Czechoslovakia (until August 17). Th Nigerian government rejects a reques from the International Red Cross for neutral airfield to be sited in Biafra.

August 16: Signing of a treaty o friendship between Romania an Czechoslovakia. The UN Security Counc unanimously condemns Israel for a raids into Jordan.

August 17: Nicolae Ceausescu pledges support for the government of Czechoslovakia.

August 20: Czechoslovakia is invaded by an army (200,000 to 600,000 strong) consisting of Soviet, Polish, Hungarian and East German troops, under the command of the Soviet Minister of Defense, General Ivan Pavlovsky. Tanks enter Prague, putting a stop to the democratization process. In the ensuing fighting, 30 people are killed and more than 300 injured.

August 21: Following the invasion of Czechoslovakia, General de Gaulle denounces bloc politics; the French Communist Party expresses surprise and, on August 22, disapproval at the intervention.

August 22: Creation of a territorial army in Romania. The Czechoslovak Communist Party holds a secret, extraordinary Congress and issues an ultimatum to the country's invaders, demanding their withdrawal within twenty-four hours. The Congress also elects a new Central Committee, to include all of the leading reformers. The new committee goes to Moscow, August 23-26, to negotiate with the Kremlin. The talks wind up when the Czechoslovak leaders obtain an assurance that Warsaw Pact troops will be withdrawn once the situation in the country has stabilized.

August 23: General Svoboda, President of the Czechoslovak Republic, arrives in Moscow. Aba, in the center of Biafra, is evacuated of all its inhabitants, civilian and military.

August 24: The first French nuclear test in the Pacific.

August 26: The Beatles launch their singles "Hey Jude" and "Revolution."

August 28: French troops go to the assistance of the government of Chad against FROLINAT (Tibesti National Liberation Front) rebels. In Mexico City, 200,000 students demonstrate to demand the resignation of the government. In East Berlin, seven young people are given long prison sentences for protesting against GDR participation in the invasion of Czechoslovakia. The

Czech national assembly unanimously condemns the continuing presence of the Soviet Army in their country as illegal and demands their withdrawal.

August 29: Vice President Humphrey is nominated as Democratic candidate for the White House.

August 30: President Johnson makes a speech aimed at preventing Soviet military intervention in Romania.

August 31: The Czechoslovak Communist Party meets to elect new leaders.

September

September 1: Censorship temporarily reimposed on press, radio and television in Czechoslovakia.

September 2: Jean-Louis Barrault loses his position as director of the Odéon theater in Paris. In Philadelphia, the third Black Power conference approves a resolution to create a black nation in five Southern States of the USA.

September 3: Official visit to Belgium by President Mobutu, his first since the Congo (now Zaïre) became independent.

September 4: In France, the restricted council of the UNR (Union for the New Republic) declares its opposition to the introduction of politics into universities. After the fall of the towns of Aba and Owerri, captured by Nigerian troops, Biafra is reduced to only one stronghold, Umuahia. The Nigerian government lifts the blockade and authorizes the Red Cross to establish an airlift.

September 5: American casualties in Vietnam since January 1, 1961 now outnumber those of the Korean War: 27,509 dead, 171,809 wounded, and 1,197 missing.

September 6: Swaziland, the last British colonial possession in Africa, becomes independent.

September 8: The French student union SNESUP encourages its members to boycott exams. Violent clashes between Israel and Egypt around the Suez Canal.

September 9: The peace talks between Biafra and Nigeria which started in Addis Ababa on August 5 are adjourned without reaching a conclusion; interna-

tional aid organizations estimate that 6,000 people die of starvation in Biafra every day.

September 10: For the first time since 1965, U.S. troops (5,000 Marines) are withdrawn from Vietnam.

September 12: Soviet troops withdraw from Prague, Brno and Bratislava. The Warsaw Pact has found a local supporter in the shape of Gustav Husak, leader of the Slovak Communist party: Husak voices his approval of the vigorous measures being taken against anti-Socialist forces. Parliamentary speaker Josef Smrkovsky travels to Moscow on September 23 to negotiate the complete withdrawal of Warsaw Pact troops. Bob Seagren, the U.S. high jump champion, beats the world record with a jump of 5.41 meters.

September 13: Censorship is reestablished in Czechoslovakia. The Soviet press judges the measures taken by the government too lenient. The Albanian government announces its intention of leaving the Warsaw Pact. Pier Paolo Pasolini's film *Theorem* wins the Premio dell Ufficio Cattolico del Cinema in Venice but is then judged to be obscene and is seized by the Italian authorities.

September 16: In spite of the fact that Biafra has been officially recognized by Tanzania, Gabon, the Ivory Coast and Zambia, the general assembly of the Organization for African Unity requests the Biafran forces to abandon their struggle for secession.

September 18: In Mexico, the army storms the university; eighteen people are killed.

September 21: The Russian automatic space station Sond 5 is recovered from the Indian Ocean, the first spacecraft to come back from the moon.

September 22: A ceremony is held in Egypt to mark the completion of the work carried out at Abu Simbel to move the temple of Rameses, which would otherwise have been submerged by the Nile. In France, elections for 103 seats in the Senate; the UDR and the Communist Party both benefit from new district boundaries in the Paris region; the center and moderate parties make gains in the provinces. Daniel Cohn-Bendit is arrested in Germany following a demonstration. In Tokyo, 1200 left-wing students try to storm the U.S. army base at Tachikawa.

September 25: "Hush," Deep Purple's first single, enters the charts.

September 26: In Portugal, Marcello Caetano, the minister for the colonies, replaces the dictator, Antonio Salazar (who has been in a coma since September 16 following a cerebral hemorrhage) as prime minister.

September 28: The Beatles launch their own record label, Apple Corps.

September 29: In Greece, a referendum for the reform of the constitution, doing away with a number of fundamental parliamentary rights, is approved by 92.2 percent of the electorate.

October

October 1: Israel rejects the peace plan put forward by the USSR, with its proposal that the four great powers monitor peace in the Middle East. The Nobel Peace Prize is awarded to the French jurist René Cassin. Marcel Duchamp dies.

October 2: The army fires on demonstrators in the Plaza de las Tres Culturas in Mexico City; about forty people are killed and one hundred wounded.

October 3: Under the watchful eye of the Soviet delegation, Warsaw Pact countries continue to negotiate the presence of their troops in Czechoslovakia with the Czech government. Alexander Dubcek, leader of the Party, and Oldrich Cernik, head of the government, are obliged to ratify a treaty with the USSR stating that the presence of Soviet troops in Czechoslovakia poses no threat to the country's national sovereignty. In spite of this, the reforms planned during the Prague spring seem to be taking shape. In France, Alain Poher is elected President of the Senate, replacing Gaston Monnerville, who did not stand for reelection. Military coup in Peru.

October 4: Ten thousand people are drowned in floods in Jaipaiguri, Bengal.

October 8: In the French National Assembly, there are 441 votes for, none against (plus 39 abstentions: 33 Communists and 6 UDR) the new bill on higher education presented by the Minister of Education, Edgar Faure; in future, higher education will be based on the principles of autonomy and participation.

October 9: In Kinshasa, execution of Pierre Mulele, leader of the Mulelist rebels and education minister in Patrice Lumumba's first government, sentenced to death on October 8.

October 10: Death of French left-wing writer and critic Jean Paulhan, at the age of 82.

October 11: Trial of dissident intellectuals in Moscow. Launch of Apollo VII, the first manned spacecraft in the U.S. Apollo series.

October 12: Opening of the 16th Olympic Games in Mexico City. The ex-Spanish colony of Equatorial Guinea gains independence. Military coup in Panama.

October 17: Nobel Prize for Literature awarded to the Japanese writer Yasunari Kawabata.

October 20: The Central Committee of the French Communist Party accepts the resignation of Jeannette Thorez-Vermeesch (in favor of Soviet intervention in Czechoslovakia) and censures Roger Garaudy (for having attacked the USSR too strongly). The Nigerian labor congress calls on the Nigerian government to break off diplomatic relations with France because the French are supplying arms to Biafra.

October 21: Violent demonstrations in Tokyo against the war in Vietnam.

October 23: Confrontation between Egyptian and Israeli aircraft over the Suez Canal.

October 26: In space, the Soviet cosmonaut Beregovoy, on board Soyuz 3, docks with Soyuz 2. Exchange of artillery fire between Egypt and Israel along 150 kilometers of the Suez Canal. In France, police search the homes of militant members of Occident, the extreme right-wing movement founded

by Pierre Sidos; the movement is banned on October 31.

October 27: The Olympic Games end with a series of triumphs for black athletes; and, perhaps to underline the revolutionary state of affairs, two black U.S. sprinters, Tommie Smith and John Carlos, gold and bronze medalists respectively in the 200 meters (on October 16), raise black-gloved fists in the Black Power salute from the podium and lower their eyes as the U.S. flag is raised. They are banned from the U.S. Olympic team. For the first time in the history of the Games, the eight finalists in the 100 meters are all black. An American, Jim Hines, wins the gold medal, equaling the world record of 9 seconds. Africans win all of the medium and long distance events. The altitude of Mexico City partly explains Bob Beamon's long jump: he demolishes the world record with a jump of 8.9 meters.

October 28: On the fiftieth anniversary of Czechoslovakian independence, thousands of young workers and students demonstrate against the Russian occupation of their country.

October 30: The Czech national assembly passes a law establishing a federal system of government.

October 31: In the USSR, test flight of the Tupolev 144, the first supersonic commercial aircraft. In China, the government proclaims the end of the Great Proletarian Cultural Revolution. In Athens, George Papandreou, the former Prime Minister, dies.

November

November 1: The Vietnam War takes a new turn as President Johnson orders a temporary halt to bombing. North Vietnam agrees to take part in negotiations if representatives of the National Liberation Front in South Vietnam (Vietcong) are also at the table. The Unites States publishes an inventory which reveals that a million tons of bombs have been dropped on 94,081 bombing missions. In addition 911 U.S. aircraft have been shot down by the Vietcong and 300 pilots taken prisoner. In Jerusalem, the Arab population stages a general strike in protest against Israeli military administration.

November 2: At its annual conference, the main French non-Communist Socialist organization, the SFIO, decides to replace its Fédération de la Gauche (Left Federation) with a new democratic Socialist party.

November 3: In France, the Prix Goncourt is awarded to Bernard Clavel for *Fruits de l'hiver*; Louis Aragon, whose own candidate François Nourissier has not been chosen, resigns from the Goncourt jury.

November 4: Richard Nixon, the Republican candidate, wins the U.S. presidential election. Hubert Humphrey obtains 42.7 percent of the vote; Nixon, 43.4 percent and the third candidate, George Wallace, just 13.5 percent. In Paris, the first four-power conference on Vietnam is adjourned. Sweden puts 1,000 soldiers at the disposal of the UN for peace-keeping in Vietnam. The Breton Liberation Front (FLB) announces that its commando activities will be halted during a visit to Brittany by General de Gaulle.

November 7: François Mitterrand resigns as president of the FGDS. Anti-Soviet demonstrations in Czechoslovakia.

November 9: The EEC agreement on the free movement of labor comes into force.

November 13: In Paris, meeting of the High School Student Action Committees at the Sorbonne.

November 18: In Czechoslovakia, reformers are expelled from the Central Committee of the Communist Party. The Czech students' strike extends to the whole country. After winning the Mexican Grand Prix in his Lotus, Graham Hill becomes world champion of Formula 1 automobile racing.

November 19: In Italy, Giovanni Leone's Christian Democrat government resigns; public sector workers strike, and disruption extends to the universities. Military coup in Mali.

November 20: The UN general assembly rejects the admission of China and the expulsion of Taiwan by 58 votes to 44, with 23 abstentions. In Madrid, Barcelona and Bilbao agitation flares up again in the universities. The linguistic status of the universities of Belgium alters.

November 22: Albert Cohen receives the Grand Prix de l'Académie française for *Belle du Seigneur*.

November 25: Marguerite Yourcenar is unanimously voted the winner of the Prix Femina for *L'Oeuvre au noir*, and Elie Wiesel is awarded the Prix Médicis for *Le Mendiant de Jérusalem*.

November 26: Under U.S. pressure, Saigon finally agrees to sit down at the negotiating table in Paris.

Décember

December 1: Israeli commandos make an incursion into Jordan. In Venezuela, Rafael Caldera is elected President of the Republic.

December 2: The UN condemns South Africa's apartheid policy. Trouble recurs in Spanish universities. The faculty of medicine in Barcelona is closed.

December 4: General strike in and around Rome. Israeli aircraft attack Iraqi positions in Jordan.

December 5: In France the National Assembly passes new legislation on trade union rights within companies.

December 8: The South Vietnamese delegation arrives in Paris for peace talks.

December 12: State of alert for the eighth anniversary of the Vietnamese NLF. Saigon fears dramatic action.

December 13: In Brazil, under pressure from the army, President Arturo da Costa e Silva dissolves parliament, seizes power and declares a military dictatorship.

December 14: Marvin Gaye launches his most successful record yet, "I Heard it Through the Grapevine," and confirms his standing as one of the greatest Afro-American singers to have emerged from Gospel.

December 15: On Okinawa, Japan, 40,000 protestors surround the U.S. air base and demand its closure.

December 16: Clashes in the faculty of letters at Nanterre (where students have been on strike since December 12 following two judicial enquiries); the Student union decides to stay on strike for as long as the police remain on campus. On December 17 the Lycée Chaptal in Paris closes; it reopens on December 20 at the insistence of its own administrative council.

December 17: François Truffaut wins the Grand Prix du Cinéma with *Baisers volés*.

December 18: In Brussels, after lengthy deliberations, the EEC agrees to adopt the Mansholt Plan for the modernization of agriculture. After eighteen months of fighting, Nigerian troops seem unable to penetrate farther into Biafran territory.

December 19: Classes resume at the Nanterre faculty of letters.

December 20: Students on strike in Rome and Madrid.

December 21: The most exciting space voyage to date starts with the launch of Apollo VIII, with U.S. astronauts Frank Borman, James A. Lovell and William Anders on board; they become the first human beings to fly over the moon. Death of John Steinbeck.

December 23: In North Korea, the crew of the U.S. spy ship Pueblo is released.

December 28: Six months after the evacuation of Khe Sanh, the Americans leave the Caroll post from which they monitored the demilitarized zone between North and South Vietnam.

LITERARY SOURCES

David Caute,
1968 in the World,
London and Paris, 1988

Eric Hobsbawm,
*Age of Extremes: The Short Twentieth
Century 1914-1991*, London 1994

Hervé Hamon and Patrick Rotman,
Génération, vol. 1 *Les Années de rêve*,
vol. 2 *Les Années de poudre*,
Paris, 1987, 1988.

Lucien Roux and René Backmann,
L'Explosion de mai, Paris, 1968

Raoul Vaneigem,
*Traité de savoir-vivre à l'usage
des jeunes générations*,
Paris, 1967

Pierre Viansson-Ponté,
Histoire de la république gaullienne,
vol. 2, *Le Temps des orphelins,
août 1962-avril 1969*, Paris, 1981

Henri Weber,
Vingt ans après que reste-t-il de 68 ?
Paris, 1988